The Ultimate Ukrainian Cookbook

111 Dishes From Ukraine To Cook Right Now

Slavka Bodic

Please sign up for free Balkan and Mediterranean recipes:
www.balkanfood.org

Introduction

Ukrainian cuisine has been renowned for its diverse flavors and memorable aromas. Its culinary culture has gained many influences from the entire Eastern Europe region, the centuries-old history of the nation, and the traditions that Slavic heritages transported. All these facets are reflected through the diversity of meals that you'll find in Ukrainian cuisine, whether the entrees, sides, desserts, drinks, breakfasts, etc. The great benefit about Ukrainian food is that it's so diverse and healthy due to the use of all nutritious ingredients like meat, fish, cabbages, potatoes, grains, etc. I know a lot of people would love to try the exotic Ukrainian flavors who are eager to recreate all its traditional recipes. And if you want the same, then look no further, as we're about to give you an exclusive collection of 111 Ukrainian Recipes in one place!

The Ultimate Ukrainian Cookbook will introduce you to Ukrainian cuisine and its vast culinary traditions in a way that you must have never tried before. It'll help you explore a variety of Ukrainian recipes. The book is great for all those beginners who are always keen to cook nutritious food and want to discover some unique flavors. With the help of this Ukrainian cuisine cookbook, you can create a complete Ukrainian menu at home, or you can cook all the special Ukrainian recipes for your own memorable celebrations.

In this book, you'll uncover popular Ukrainian meals and ones that you might not have heard of formerly. From nourishing dishes, breakfast hash, to all of the soups, desserts, drinks, main dishes, and salads, you can find them all. Plus, all these Ukrainian recipes are created in such a simple way that those who aren't quite familiar with the Ukrainian culture, food, and language can still try and cook them at home with complete ease and absolute convenience.

In fact, Ukrainian cuisine is full of flavorsome surprises that bring you a blend of all Eastern European culinary traditions. So, if you want to add all those amazing meals to your menu, then give this book a thorough read, and you'll discover all the right answers in one place.

Here's what you can find in this cookbook:

- Facts about the Ukraine and Ukrainian Cuisine
- Ukrainian Breakfast Recipes
- The Snacks, Sides, or Appetizers
- Main Dishes
- Ukrainian Desserts and Drinks

Let's prepare all these Ukrainian Recipes and recreate a complete menu to celebrate the amazing Ukrainian flavors and aromas.

Table of Contents

INTRODUCTION 3

WHY UKRAINIAN CUISINE? 9

UKRAINE 11

BREAKFAST 13

    UKRAINIAN BREAKFAST HASH 14

    UKRAINIAN BREAKFAST SANDWICH 16

    UKRAINIAN VILLAGE BREAKFAST 18

    UKRAINIAN BREAKFAST POTATOES WITH BACON 19

    UKRAINIAN GARLIC BREAD (PAMPUSHKI) 20

    UKRAINIAN CHRISTMAS BREAD (KULICH) 22

    BUBLIK 24

    UKRAINIAN PANCAKES (DERUNY) 26

    UKRAINIAN SYRNIKI 28

    FISH BUTTER 29

    SEMOLINA PORRIDGE 30

    FLUFFY PANCAKES 31

APPETIZERS 32

    POTATO PAMPUSHKI 33

    ROASTED EGGPLANT DIP 35

    EGGPLANT ROLL UP APPETIZER 36

    GARLIC CHEESE 37

    SALMON TOAST 38

    CHICKEN POTATO CUTLET 39

    PELMENI DUMPLINGS 41

    PICKLE HERRING 43

    VARENIKI 45

SALADS 47

    UKRAINIAN SALAT VINAIGRETTE (BEET SALAD) 48

    OLIVYE SALAD (UKRAINIAN POTATO SALAD) 49

    TOMATO AND CUCUMBER SALAD 50

    UKRAINIAN ICEBERG SALAD 51

    LEEK SALAD WITH APPLES AND CARROTS 52

    CREAMY UKRAINIAN SALAD 53

POTATO SALAD 54

SOUR CREAM CUCUMBER SALAD 55

SALAD WITH TONGUE AND BRYNDZA 56

GARDEN SALAD 57

SOUPS **58**

UKRAINIAN CHICKEN SOUP 59

POTATO EGG SOUP 61

BEAN SOUP WITH WALNUTS 62

PEA SOUP 63

UKRAINIAN RED BORSCHT SOUP 64

UKRAINIAN CABBAGE SOUP 66

UKRAINIAN MUSHROOM SOUP 68

VEGETABLE SOUP 69

UKRAINIAN BEETROOT BROTH (BORSCH) 71

UKRAINIAN POTATO SOUP 72

UKRAINIAN GREEN BORSCH (SORREL SOUP) 73

POTATO PORK MILLET SOUP (KAPUSTNYAK ZAPORIZHIAN) 75

CHICKEN SOLYANKA SOUP 77

UKRAINIAN MUSHROOM AND POTATO SOUP 79

UKRAINIAN GREEN BEAN AND POTATO SOUP 81

MAIN DISHES **82**

CABBAGE MEAT STEW 83

CABBAGE PIE 84

UKRAINIAN PORK ROAST 85

BEEF STROGANOFF 86

STUFFED CABBAGE 88

CHICKEN KIEV 90

CHICKEN POTATO STEW 92

VERENIKE CASSEROLE 93

KARTOSHNIK WITH CHEESE AND ONIONS 94

UKRAINIAN PIROSHKI 95

UKRAINIAN CHICKEN STEW 97

UKRAINIAN SHASHLIK 99

MUSHROOM JULIENNE 100

PORK SOLYANKA 101

GRILLED TROUT 102

CHEESE FISH 103

SHASHLIK 104

CHICKEN SHASHLIK 105

Lamb Shashlik 106

Steamed Salmon 108

Mushroom Caviar 110

Ukrainian Pie 111

Ukrainian Chicken Pie 112

Ukrainian Lamb Rice 114

Potato Turnip Stew 116

Ukrainian Kotletki 117

Pork Loin Steaks 118

Ukrainian Chicken Rice 120

Turkey Kotleti 121

Chicken Kotleti 122

Chicken Cabbage Pirog 124

Clam Stew 126

Buckwheat Mushroom Croquettes 128

Fish Ukha 130

Chicken and Beef Croquettes 131

Turkey Kotleti with Mushroom Filling 133

Potatoes in A Garlic Cream Sauce 135

Chicken Butter Kiev 136

Stuffed Cabbage Rolls (Golubtsi) 138

Chicken Tenders 140

Trout with Parsley Butter 142

Pork Tefteli In A Cream Sauce 143

Potatoes with Pork 145

DESSERTS 147

Ukrainian Apple Cake (Yabluchnyk) 148

Ukrainian Honey Babka 150

Ukrainian Honey Cake 152

Ukrainian Sweet Cheese 153

Kulich 154

Traditional Donuts 156

Khrustyky 158

Ukrainian Cheesecake Tarts 159

Ukrainian Walnut Torte 160

Ukrainian Kutia 162

Ukrainian Prune Torte 163

Cheese Pockets 165

Strawberry Cake 167

Plum Cake 168

Ukrainian Cookies 169

Ukrainian Biscottis 170

Spicy Cookies 172

DRINKS... **174**

Apple Kvass 175

Kompot Drink 176

Ukrainian Mulled Wine.. 177

Uzvar... 178

Beetroot Drink 179

ONE LAST THING **188**

Why Ukrainian Cuisine?

Ukrainian cuisine is unique and exotic in the sense that it brings all the traditional East European recipes and the modern European culinary culture together. It has a collection of all the historic cooking traditions that were passed down from generation to generation in that region. This cuisine shares many commonalities with the Russian cuisine as Ukraine was once a part of the Russian region. And for this reason you'll locate several of the Russian recipes under the Ukrainian menu. In these recipes, there's great use of certain vegetables like:

- Cabbages
- Potatoes
- Mushrooms
- Beetroots

The cuisine has diverse flavors and incorporates all type of food containing carbohydrates, fats, protein, vegetables, fruits, and soups. The climatic condition of Ukraine calls for the use of soups in everyday cuisine. There are certain soup recipes that are very famous in this region, like borsch. These soups are prepared using vegetables, pork, cabbage, pickled cucumbers, mushrooms, catfish, and several other ingredients.

Besides soups, there are salads and appetizers that you'll deem as delicious and interesting in Ukrainian cuisine. In the salads, there's widespread use of potatoes, onion, peas, boiled eggs, pickles, vegetables, carrots, onions, etc.

Plus, there's a great variety of bread and celebratory products in Ukrainian cuisine. Babka is famous Easter bread that's enjoyed on all occasions. For instance, Bublik is a ring-shaped bread made from savory dough. Kulich is a typical Ukrainian ring-shaped bread, which is served at funerals and Christmas. Then comes Paska and other breads that are very famous and popular in the region.

Among the popular main courses, you'll find chicken Kyiv, which is a stuffed chicken recipe. Then, there's a great use of roasted meat, stuffed duck, Fish, goulash, and potato pancakes in the Ukrainian cuisine. In desserts, you'll also acquire some interesting combination of ingredients like honey, nuts, wheat, and poppy seed. In traditional dishes called Katia, Pampushki are some of the famous Ukrainian desserts. In drinks, you can have the finest mulled wine and Kvass, which use the best of fermented apple extracts.

Ukraine

Ukraine remains in the news all the time. And it's a country that everyone is quite familiar with. But do you know that Ukraine was the birthplace of the Russian Empire? Kyiv city was the first-ever region that was ruled by the East Slavic and Uralic people in this part of Europe. Ukraine has a great history and still owns a significant place in the world's stage. The state is located in Eastern Europe, neighboring Russia on its Northeastern border. Ukraine also shares its borders with Hungary, Slovakia, Poland, and Belarus. It has Moldova and Romania to the South, and its coastline touches the bed of the Azov Sea and the Black Sea.

The country has more than 45 million people. It's also considered the eighth-most populous country in Europe. Kyiv is the largest city in the country by land area. Ukraine is the second-largest European country after Russia. It covers a large area of and its landscape consists of plateaus, fertile plains, and rivers.

Ukraine is a geographically diverse region, with all the highlands and lowlands. It has the Carpathian Mountains in the West and the Crimean Mountains in Crimea. The region has significant natural resources, including timber, mercury, nickel, Guilin, magnesium, titanium graphite, sulfur, salt, oil, natural gas, manganese coal, and iron ore. Ukraine usually experiences a temperate climate, except for its Southern Coast of Crimea, where the climate is subtropical. It remains moderately warm due to the humid air coming from the Atlantic

Ocean. The precipitation is high in the West and lowest in the East and in the Southeast.

Like other great countries of Europe, Ukraine also provides major tourist attractions, including:

- The Pottery Museum. This museum was founded by one of the oldest potter's families in Ukraine.
- Then there's a local history museum in Poltava, which showcases all the historical architecture of Ukraine.
- One of the biggest pilgrimage locations of Hasidic Jews, the Hasidic Judaism Center, is also located in Ukraine.
- Kyiv Caves-Lavra
- St. Sophia's Cathedral
- St. Michael's Golden-Domed Monastery
- Motherland Monument
- Independence Squares
- St. Andrew's Church
- Golden Gate
- Tunnel of Love

The Tunnel Love has the most stunning view. It's actually a section of an industrial railway that's no longer in use. The whole tunnel is covered with green arches which extend up to 2 miles. It's a great place for walking and photography.

Breakfast

Ukrainian Breakfast Hash

Preparation time: 15 minutes
Cook time: 38 minutes
Nutrition facts (per serving): 352 Cal (15g fat, 24g protein, 4g fiber)

This breakfast hash brings you a hearty meal to start your day. The hash is best to serve with crispy bread and bacon.

Ingredients (6 servings)
10 Yukon gold potatoes, chopped
2 tablespoon baby dill, chopped
1 onion, chopped
⅔ cup sauerkraut liquid
1 ½ Ukrainian sausage, sliced
2 ½ cups mushrooms, sliced
1 green pepper, chopped
2 tablespoon vegetable oil
3 tablespoon butter
1 cup dry cottage cheese
2 garlic cloves crushed
1 teaspoon salt
½ teaspoon black pepper

Garnish
Dollop sour cream
Sprigs fresh dill

Preparation

Sauté the kielbasa with oil in a large skillet for 4 minutes and put it aside. Sauté the onions, garlic, and green peppers with 1 tablespoon oil in the same skillet for 5 minutes, and then add mushrooms, sauté for 4 minutes, and then transfer to a bowl. Sauté the potatoes with butter in the same skillet for 15 minutes, add the cheese, sauerkraut, kielbasa, and onion mixture, and then sauté for 10 minutes. Garnish with fresh dill and sour cream. Serve warm.

Ukrainian Breakfast Sandwich

Preparation time: 5 minutes
Cook time: 5 minutes
Nutrition facts (per serving): 205 Cal (11.8g fat, 10g protein, 2g fiber)

This Ukrainian breakfast sandwich is a typical Ukrainian breakfast, which is a must on the menu. It has this rich mix of egg with cottage cheese and sour cream.

Ingredients (2 servings)

1 egg
1 tablespoon dry cottage cheese
½ teaspoon dill
1 tablespoon sour cream
⅓ cup Ukrainian kielbasa, sliced
1 teaspoon mustard
½ teaspoon horseradish
1 whole-wheat English muffin
2 tomato slices

Preparation

At 425 degrees F, preheat your oven. Sauté the garlic and the onions with oil in a skillet until soft. Toast the English muffin. Grease a coffee mug with nonstick cooking spray. Break the egg into this mug and then add the dry cottage cheese and the dill on top. Cook this egg mixture in the microwave for 40 seconds. Run the knife around the egg to lose it. Mix the horseradish, sour cream, and mustard together. Spread this cream mixture on each side of the English muffin. Top one side of the English muffin with kielbasa and the cooked egg. Add the sliced tomato and another half of the English muffin. Serve fresh.

Ukrainian Village Breakfast

Preparation time: 5 minutes
Cook time: 16 minutes
Nutrition facts (per serving): 520 Cal (32g fat, 43g protein, 0g fiber)

Simple and easy to make, this recipe is a must on this menu. Lardo mixed with eggs, kale, and chicken are delightful for the breakfast table.

Ingredients (4 servings)
2 oz. cured slabs of fatback (lardo), chopped
1 shallot, sliced
1 free-range chicken breast, thinly sliced
3 ½ oz. kale
4 medium eggs

Preparation
Sauté the lardo in a suitable frying pan for 5 minutes. Stir in the shallot and cook for 4 minutes. Add the chicken to the skillet and cook for 2 minutes. Toss in the kale and continue cooking for 5 minutes, make some space for eggs and crack eggs in each space in the mixture, and add the seasoning on the top. Scramble and cook until the eggs are set. Serve warm.

Ukrainian Breakfast Potatoes with Bacon

Preparation time: 5 minutes
Cook time: 20 minutes
Nutrition facts (per serving): 445 Cal (21g fat, 60g protein, 4g fiber)

Potatoes with bacon offer a simpler variety of hash. This one is easy and quick to make in the morning. You can serve these potatoes with fried or poached eggs.

Ingredients (4 servings)

2 lbs. red potatoes, peeled and cubed
6 thin bacon slices chopped
1 tablespoon olive oil
½ teaspoon salt
Black pepper, to taste

Preparation

Sauté the bacon in a suitable cooking pan for 7 minutes and transfer the crispy bacon to a plate lined with a paper towel. Add the potatoes, black pepper, and salt, to the same pan, and cook for 10 minutes, with occasional stirring. Add the oil and continue cooking for 10 minutes. Remove that pan from the heat and add the fried bacon and the salt on top. Serve the potatoes with fried or poached eggs on top.

Ukrainian Garlic Bread (Pampushki)

Preparation time: 15 minutes
Cook time: 25 minutes
Nutrition facts (per serving): 256 Cal (5.2g fat, 3g protein, 18g fiber)

Have you tried the garlicky version of Pampushki bread for breakfast? Well, here's a Ukrainian delight that adds exotic flavors to your morning meal in a delicious way.

Ingredients (4 servings)

2 ¼ teaspoon active dry yeast
1 teaspoon granulated sugar
1 cup warm water
2 ½ cups white bread flour
1 ½ teaspoon fine sea salt

Topping

3 tablespoon sunflower oil
4 garlic cloves, minced
2 tablespoon fresh parsley, chopped
1 pinch salt
1 egg beaten

Preparation

Add yeast, warm water, and sugar to a suitable mixing bowl. Mix well and leave for 10 minutes. Add the bread flour to this mixture with the salt. Mix well and knead this dough on the working surface until smooth. Place this dough in a greased bowl and cover with plastic wrap.

Leave it for one hour, punch down the dough, and divide it into eight equal pieces. Roll out each piece into a ball. And again, leave these balls in a baking pan.

At 425-degree Fahrenheit, preheat your oven. Mix garlic, three tablespoon oil, parsley, and salt in a small bowl. Place the dough balls on a suitable baking pan. Brush them with the garlic mixture and the beaten egg. Then bake them for 25 minutes. Add the remaining garlic oil on top and serve warm.

Ukrainian Christmas Bread (Kulich)

Preparation time: 15 minutes
Cook time: 60 minutes
Nutrition facts (per serving): 213 Cal (20g fat, 9g protein, 7g fiber)

The Ukrainian Christmas bread or Kulich is famous for its delicious combination of basic bread ingredients and its soft and moist texture.

Ingredients (6 servings)
Yeast
1 (¼-oz.) package active dry yeast
1 teaspoon sugar
⅓ cup lukewarm water
3 large eggs

Dough
2 tablespoon sugar
2 tablespoon oil
1 teaspoon salt
½ cup lukewarm water
4 cups all-purpose flour

Egg wash
1 egg yolk
1 teaspoon water

Preparation

Mix the yeast with sugar and lukewarm water in a suitable bowl and leave it for 15 minutes. Meanwhile, add the eggs to a mixing bowl and beat well. Stir in the yeast mixture, oil sugar, and salt. Then mix well. Add two cups of flour and the remaining ingredients. Mix well and knead the dough until smooth. Transfer this dough to a greased bowl, cover it with plastic wrap, and leave it for one hour. Punch down the dough and divide it into three equal pieces. Roll each piece into our long, thick rope. Pinch the three ropes together at one end and braid them together.

Take a 10-inch loaf pan, and grease it with cooking oil. Brush the braided dough with your wash and place it in the prepared pan. Bake this braided bread for 60 minutes at 350 degrees Fahrenheit in the preheated oven. Serve warm.

Bublik

Preparation time: 10 minutes
Cook time: 22 minutes
Nutrition facts (per serving): 478 Cal (16g fat, 14g protein, 2g fiber)

Bublik is a type of Ukrainian breakfast donut. It tastes heavenly when cooked and baked at home. Serve warm with your favorite toppings and bacon on the side.

Ingredients (6 servings)

1¾ cups milk
½ cup butter
5 tablespoon caster sugar
2 eggs
3 ½ cups flour
2 tablespoon active dry yeast
1 tablespoon salt
2 tablespoon milk
Poppy seeds
Sesame seeds

Preparation

Add the milk, butter, and half of the sugar to a saucepan and let this mixture to boil; remove the mixture from the heat, add the yeast, and leave for 20 minutes. Meanwhile, mix remaining the sugar and flour in a bowl and stir in the egg whites. Mix well using the dough hook of the stand mixer. Stir in the yeast mixture and mix well until it makes smooth dough. Cover this dough with a cloth and leave it. Punch down this dough and divide into 30 equal pieces. Roll each piece into a half-inch thick and five inches in diameter circle. Make a hole at the center of each circle.

At 390 degrees Fahrenheit, preheat your oven. Add water to a suitable saucepan and boil it. Dip each ball in this boiling water for 20 seconds and then remove it immediately, using a slotted spoon. Place the boiled balls on the baking sheet lined with parchment paper and brush them with the egg yolk and milk mixture drizzle, sesame, or poppy seeds on top, and bake these balls for 20 minutes. Serve fresh.

Ukrainian Pancakes (Deruny)

Preparation time: 15 minutes
Cook time: 10 minutes
Nutrition facts (per serving): 256 Cal (16g fat, 9g protein, 6g fiber)

These potato pancakes are another nutritious yet simple meal for the breakfast table. They add lots of nutrients and fibers to the table, along with healthy ingredients that are cooked together in a tempting combination.

Ingredients (4 servings)
4 large Yukon potatoes
1 small yellow onion
1 large egg
3 tablespoon all-purpose flour
1 teaspoon fine salt or to taste
¼ teaspoon baking soda
Grapeseed oil for frying

Preparation
Grate the onions and the potatoes using a grater, place their shreds in a colander, and leave them for 10 minutes. Next, squeeze out the excess potato and onion juices and transfer the vegetables to a suitable bowl. Mix the flour, egg, salt, and baking soda in another bowl; add enough water to make thick dough. Stir in the potatoes and the onions and mix well.

Place a suitable pan over medium-high heat, grease it with cooking oil and pour one tablespoon of the potato mixture. Spread it into a pancake and cook for two-three minutes per side. Make more pancakes in the same way. Serve fresh.

Ukrainian Syrniki

Preparation time: 15 minutes

Cook time: 10 minutes

Nutrition facts (per serving): 410 Cal (6g fat, 10g protein, 1.4g fiber)

Try the Ukrainian Syrniki for your breakfast, which is made from cheese, eggs, and flour batter. The recipe is simple and gives lots of nutrients in one place.

Ingredients (4 servings)

2 cups farmer's cheese

4 large eggs

¾ cups all-purpose flour

3 tablespoon sugar

½ teaspoon salt

1 teaspoon baking soda

1 teaspoon white vinegar

1 cup raisins

3 tablespoon olive oil

Preparation

Mix the eggs, cheese, ¾ cup flour, sugar, and salt in the suitable bowl Stir in baking soda and vinegar and mix well until smooth. Fold in the raisins and keep this mixture aside. Set a suitable pan over medium heat, with three tablespoon olive oil. Spread half cup flour in a small bowl. Take a tablespoon of cheese mixture using a small ice cream scooper and coat this cheese ball with flour. In the bowl, shake off the excess and press the ball into a small patty. Sear each patty for three to four minutes per side. Garnish with sour cream, powdered sugar, and fruit.

Fish Butter

Preparation time: 10 minutes

Nutrition facts (per serving): 225 Cal (17g fat, 13g protein, 1.2g fiber)

If you want to make a perfect toast spread for breakfast, then this smoked fish butter spread is everything you should go for.

Ingredients (10 servings)

10 ½ oz. hot-smoked trout, skin removed

⅔ inch-piece horseradish root, peeled and grated

2 tablespoon unsalted butter softened

2 tablespoon thick cream

2 hard-boiled eggs

Juice of ½ lemon

Salt and black pepper, to taste

Preparation

Crumble the smoked fish into a bowl to get the flakes. Stir in the remaining ingredients and mash with a fork until smooth. Cover the mixture with a plastic sheet and refrigerate for 1 hour. Serve as a breakfast on top of the bread slices.

Semolina Porridge

Preparation time: 15 minutes
Cook time: 5 minutes
Nutrition facts (per serving): 148 Cal (5.5g fat, 5.8g protein, 0.5g fiber)

Semolina porridge is full of energy and nutrients, and you can get it ready in no time. The combination of milk with semolina gives it a super creamy texture.

Ingredients (2 servings)
⅓ cup of semolina flour
1 pint of milk
1 tablespoon of butter
1 tablespoon of sugar
Salt, to taste
Seedless berry jam, to serve

Preparation
Mix the milk with sugar and butter in a saucepan and place it over high heat to boil. Stir well and then remove it from the heat. Stir in the semolina flour, mix well, and return the pan to the heat. Cook again until the mixture thickens. Serve.

Fluffy Pancakes

Preparation time: 15 minutes
Cook time: 10 minutes
Nutrition facts (per serving): 241 Cal (3.3g fat, 9.8g protein, 1.2g fiber)

The Oladi pancakes are the fluffiest pancakes that you can find. Try them for breakfast and keep their batter ready in the refrigerator.

Ingredients (4 servings)
2 cup flour
3 eggs
2 cup buttermilk
1 tablespoon baking powder
½ teaspoon salt
3 tablespoon sugar
Canola oil, for frying

Preparation
Beat the eggs with buttermilk, salt, and sugar in a mixing bowl. Stir in the flour and the baking powder and then mix until lump-free. Place a pan over medium heat and add a tablespoon of oil for cooking. Add 2 tablespoon of the batter, spread it evenly, and cook for 2 minutes per side until golden brown. Make more pancakes using the remaining batter. Serve.

Appetizers

Potato Pampushki

Preparation time: 5 minutes
Cook time: 10 minutes
Nutrition facts (per serving): 231 Cal (20g fat, 22g protein, 6g fiber)

Here comes the potato mixed Pampushki recipe. You can try serving them as snacks, sides, or appetizers. Enjoy them with your favorite sauce.

Ingredients (8 servings)
¾ lb. potatoes, peeled and grated
1 cup potatoes mashed
½ teaspoon salt
⅛ teaspoon black pepper
½ cup feta
2 tablespoon chives snipped
1 cup flour
1 large egg
1 teaspoon water
1 cup breadcrumbs

Preparation
Squeeze the grated potatoes in a cheesecloth to remove excess water. Mix the mashed potatoes with salt and black pepper in a suitable bowl. Mix the cheese and the chives in another bowl. Take a scoop of potatoes mixture and spread it over your palm. Add 2 teaspoon cheese filling on top and fold the edges then roll in to a ball. Make more balls in the same way. Coat these balls with flour, beat with the eggs, and finally with the

breadcrumbs. Deep fry these balls in oil for 10 minutes until golden brown. Remove using a slotted spoon and serve.

Roasted Eggplant Dip

Preparation time: 10 minutes
Cook time: 30 minutes
Nutrition facts (per serving): 289 Cal (13g fat, 6.8g protein, 3g fiber)

This eggplant dip will melt your heart away with its great flavors. The eggplant is first roasted and then blended with other ingredients to make this delectable dip.

Ingredients (8 servings)

2 medium eggplants, halved
1 large tomato
1 large garlic clove, chopped
3 tablespoons red onion, chopped
3 tablespoons parsley, chopped
3 tablespoons sunflower oil
1 ½ teaspoons salt
¼ teaspoon ground black pepper

Preparation

Poke the eggplants with a fork and rub them with oil. Place them on a baking sheet and bake for 30 minutes at 400 degrees F. Cut the tomato in half and squeeze out the juice. Peel the roasted eggplant and blend with the rest of the ingredients in a blender. Serve.

Eggplant Roll Up Appetizer

Preparation time: 15 minutes
Cook time: 10 minutes
Nutrition facts (per serving): 294 cal (9g fat, 20g protein, 0.7g fiber)

If you haven't tried these eggplant appetizers before, then here comes a simple and easy to cook recipe that you can recreate at home in no time with minimum efforts.

Ingredients (4 servings)

2 medium eggplants, sliced
1 large carrot, shredded
1 large scallion, shredded
1 garlic head, peeled and minced
1 tablespoon oil
3 tablespoon tomato paste
1 tablespoon mayonnaise
Salt and black pepper, to taste

Preparation

Sauté the carrots, garlic, scallion, and garlic with oil in a skillet for 5 minutes until soft. Stir the tomato paste, mayonnaise, black pepper, and salt. Mix well and cook for 5 minutes. Spread eggplant slices in a greased baking sheet and divide the carrots mixture at the bottom of each eggplant slice. Roll these slices and serve.

Garlic Cheese

Preparation time: 5 minutes
Nutrition facts (per serving): 139 Cal (11.5g fat, 7.1g protein, 0g fiber)

The garlic cheese is one of the most loved Ukrainian side and appetizer meals, and it can be served with all types of crackers and crispy delights.

Ingredients (8 servings)

8 oz. Havarti cheese, shredded
2 garlic cloves, minced
4 tablespoon mayonnaise
2 tablespoon green onion, chopped
4 tablespoon radicchios, chopped
1 pinch salt
1 pinch black pepper

Preparation

Mix the cheese with the garlic, mayonnaise, green onion, radicchio, salt, and black pepper in a bowl. Refrigerate for 1 hour then serve.

Salmon Toast

Preparation time: 10 minutes
Nutrition facts (per serving): 206 Cal (14.6g fat, 7.7g protein, 1.2g fiber)

The smoked salmon served on the Ukrainian rye bread is a delight for every table, and it provides all the essential nutrients.

Ingredients (4 servings)
1 dark rye bread
8 oz. spreadable cream cheese
5 oz. smoked salmon
Fresh dill

Preparation
Cut 2 inches round from the rye bread using a cookie cutter. Mix the salmon with the cream cheese and dill in a mixing bowl. Top the rye bread rounds with the salmon mixture. Serve.

Chicken Potato Cutlet

Preparation time: 15 minutes

Cook time: 30 minutes

Nutrition facts (per serving):207 Cal (2.1g fat, 28.3g protein, 1.7g fiber)

Try these potato cutlets as appetizers or as a snack; in any case, they'll add a much-needed twist of crisp to your menu.

Ingredients (4 servings)

4 potatoes

10 ½ oz. boneless chicken

1 tablespoon ginger garlic paste

1 tablespoon green chili paste

1 teaspoon black pepper powder

½ teaspoon soya sauce

1 teaspoon vinegar

1 tablespoon green chili sauce

2 cheese cubes

Salt, to taste

2 tablespoon capsicum

2 tablespoon carrot

2 tablespoon coriander leaves

1 cup edible oil

1 egg whisked with 1 teaspoon of milk

Preparation

Boil the potatoes in the salted water until soft and transfer them to a bowl. Mash the potatoes with a fork. Add the chicken, green chili sauce, vinegar, soya sauce, salt, and ginger garlic paste to the saucepan. Cook until the chicken is done and then shred it with two forks. Add the shredded chicken to the mashed potatoes and then mix well. Sauté the carrot and the capsicum in a greased skillet. Transfer the veggies to the mashed potatoes and then mix well. Stir in the cheese and the coriander leaves. Then mix well and make small cutlets from this mixture. Set a skillet with cooking oil over medium heat. Sear the cutlets in the oil until golden brown from both sides. Serve.

Pelmeni Dumplings

Preparation time: 15 minutes

Cook time: 10 minutes

Nutrition facts (per serving): 255 Cal (5g fat, 18.5g protein, 1.5g fiber)

Make your menu more diverse by adding these pelmeni dumplings. They're quite popular in authentic Ukrainian cuisine.

Ingredients (8 servings)

Dough

2 large eggs

⅔ cup water

1 tablespoon vegetable oil

½ teaspoon salt

3 ¼ cups flour

Filling

1 large onion, grated

8 oz. lean, ground pork

8 oz. ground beef

1 ½ teaspoon salt

½ teaspoon black pepper

Preparation

Beat the eggs with water, vegetable oil, salt, and flour in a mixing bowl until it makes smooth dough. Knead the dough for 5 minutes and wrap the dough with a plastic wrap. Leave this dough for 30 minutes.

Meanwhile, make the filling and mix the ground beef with black pepper and salt in a mixing bowl. Cover and refrigerate the filling for 1 hour. Divide the prepared dough into 8 equal-sized pieces. Roll one piece into a log, but keep the remaining dough pieces in the refrigerator. Cut the log into 10 equal pieces and press the dough pieces into 2 inched circles. Add a teaspoon of the beef filling to each circle and pinch the edges of the dough circles to make the dumplings. Boil salted water in a saucepan and add the dumplings. Cook them for 2 minutes in the salted water. Serve warm.

Pickle Herring

Preparation time: 10 minutes
Cook time: 10 minutes
Nutrition facts (per serving): 207 Cal (14g fat, 17g protein, 1g fiber)

The simplest of the pickle herring rolls can make your Ukrainian menu super special because of their juicy and tart taste.

Ingredients (8 servings)

4 whole salt herrings
2 tablespoon black pepper
2 tablespoon grainy Polish mustard
1 large onion, chopped
2 medium pickles, quartered
½ cup white vinegar
1 cup of water
1 bay leaf
3 tablespoon vegetable oil
Pinch sugar

Preparation

Soak the herrings in a pan filled with cold water for 24 hours. Change the fish water every 3 hours. Clean the fish inside out and remove all the scales, bone, and innards. Rub each herring with mustard, onion, and black pepper. Add a pickle on top of the fish, roll the fish around the pickle, and then insert the toothpick to seal. Set a saucepan over medium heat. Add water, vinegar, bay leaf, and remaining onion. Cook the mixture to a boil then strain. Stir in the sugar, oil, and seasonings.

Place the rolled herring in a sealable container and pour in the vinegar mixture. Cover and refrigerate overnight. Serve.

Vareniki

Preparation time: 5 minutes

Cook time: 15 minutes

Nutrition facts (per serving): 361 Cal (20g fat, 11g protein, 0.8g fiber)

Have you ever tried the famous Vareniki dumplings before? Well, here come the cheese- packed dumplings which can be served with all sorts of dips and sauces.

Ingredients (6 servings)

Dough

6 cups flour

½ pint sour cream

¼ lb. butter

¾ cup milk

1 tablespoon salt

4 eggs

Filling

1 lb. cottage cheese

1 egg yolks

¼ teaspoon black pepper

½ teaspoon salt

Preparation

Whisk the cottage cheese with egg yolk, black pepper and salt in a bowl. Mix the sour cream, melted butter, and milk in a saucepan and heat it.

Beat the eggs with flour and salt in a bowl and then add the sour cream mixture. Mix well and knead this dough. Divide this dough in half and spread it into a circle. Add the sour cream filling at the center of the dough, fold in half and press the edges. Add water to a cooking pot and boil it. Add the dumplings to the water and cook for 5 minutes. Remove from the heat and serve.

Salads

Ukrainian Salat Vinaigrette (Beet Salad)

Preparation time: 15 minutes
Cook time: 30 minutes
Nutrition facts (per serving): 423 Cal (6g fat, 38g protein, 0g fiber)

The Ukrainian salat Vinaigrette goes perfectly with all the Ukrainian entrees. This recipe will add a lot of appeal and color to your dinner table.

Ingredients (4 servings)

1 lb. beets
1 lb. carrots
1 lb. potatoes
2 large dill pickles, diced
1 onion, minced
1 (8 oz.) can peas, drained
2 tablespoon olive oil
½ teaspoon black pepper
1 tablespoon fresh parsley, chopped
½ teaspoon salt

Preparation

Boil the beets with water in a suitable saucepan then cook for 20 minutes on a simmer. Add the potatoes and carrots and cook 10 minutes. Remove from the heat and leave the veggies covered overnight. Peel and dice all the veggies and mix well in a salad bowl. Serve.

Olivye Salad (Ukrainian Potato Salad)

Preparation time: 15 minutes
Nutrition facts (per serving): 378 Cal (11g fat, 33g protein, 1.2g fiber)

The Ukrainian Potato salad is here to complete your Ukrainian menu. Its fiber-rich content makes it super healthy and nutritious.

Ingredients (4 servings)

2 large Yukon potatoes, cooked and diced
2 large carrots, cooked, chopped
7 boiled eggs, peeled and diced
9 pickles, chopped
1 (15 oz.) Ballpark chicken, cooked and diced
1 large yellow onion
1 (15 oz.) canned sweet peas
Mayonnaise for dressing
Fresh parsley for garnish

Preparation

Mix the chicken, pickles, and all the ingredients in a salad bowl. Serve.

Tomato and Cucumber Salad

Preparation time: 10 minutes
Nutrition facts (per serving): 392 Cal (19g fat, 25g protein, 2g fiber)

The tomato and cucumber salad are here to add flavors to your dinner table, but this time with a mix of vegetables, dill, and sour cream.

Ingredients (4 servings)

2 medium size tomatoes
4 baby cucumbers
½ of small red onion
1-2 garlic cloves
Fresh dill, to taste
3 tablespoons of sour cream
2 tablespoon of mayonnaise
Ground pepper, to taste
Salt, to taste

Preparation

Mix the tomatoes with cucumber and rest of the ingredients in a salad bowl. Serve.

Ukrainian Iceberg Salad

Preparation time: 10 minutes
Nutrition facts (per serving): 127 Cal (11g fat, 1g protein, 2.1g fiber)

This iceberg salad is the best in Ukrainian cuisine. This salad is loaded with nutrients as it's prepared with lettuce, eggs, mayo dressing, and cucumber.

Ingredients (4 servings)
1 iceberg lettuce
2-3 cucumbers, sliced
2 boiled eggs, peeled and sliced
1 bunch fresh herbs, chopped

Dressing
4 tablespoon mayonnaise
3 tablespoon French mustard
Salt, to taste

Preparation
Spread the lettuce and other salad ingredients on a platter. Mix the dressing ingredients and pour over the salad. Serve.

Leek Salad with Apples and Carrots

Preparation time: 10 minutes
Nutrition facts (per serving): 156 Cal (3.5g fat, 5.7g protein, 2g fiber)

The leek and apple salad offers another most popular salad in Ukrainian cuisine, and it has this great taste from the mix of carrots, apples, and mayo.

Ingredients (4 servings)

1 large leeks, diced
1 large carrots, peeled and grated
1 apple, cored and cut into matchsticks
¼ cup vegan mayo
¼ teaspoon fine sea salt
Freshly black pepper, to taste

Preparation

Mix the carrots, the apple, and the rest of the ingredients in a salad bowl. Serve.

Creamy Ukrainian Salad

Preparation time: 10 minutes
Cook time: 5 minutes
Nutrition facts (per serving): 211 Cal (20g fat, 4g protein, 13g fiber)

The creamy Ukrainian salad is the right fit to serve with all your Ukrainian entrees. Here the cucumbers and radishes are mixed with dill and cottage cheese, which makes a great combination.

Ingredients (4 servings)
2 medium cucumbers, peeled and sliced
1 bunch of radishes, sliced
1 bunch of scallions, chopped
Fresh dill, chopped
1 cup of cottage cheese
Salt and black pepper, to taste
2 garlic cloves, minced

Preparation
Boil the carrots in a pot filled with salted water until soft. Drain and transfer the carrots to a salad bowl. Stir in the radishes, red peppers, and olives and then mix well. Add the olive oil, lemon juice, parsley, salt, cinnamon, black pepper, and garlic in a small bowl. Pour this prepared mixture over the veggies and mix well. Cover and refrigerate for 30 minutes. Serve.

Potato Salad

Preparation time: 10 minutes
Nutrition facts (per serving): 253 Cal (2g fat, 21g protein, 4g fiber)

Here comes a delicious and healthy salad, which has a refreshing twist due to the use of potatoes and kielbasa in it. It's great to serve with beef skewers and kebabs.

Ingredients (6 servings)

12 oz. smoked kielbasa, cooked
8 oz. bologna, cooked and diced
3 large potatoes, cooked and diced
5 medium carrots, diced
½ small onion
6 boiled eggs, peeled and diced
1 can sweet peas
5 medium pickles, diced
½ English cucumber, chopped
2 cups mayonnaise
Salt and black pepper, to taste

Preparation

Mix the potatoes, eggs, and the rest of the ingredients in a salad bowl. Serve.

Sour Cream Cucumber Salad

Preparation time: 10 minutes
Nutrition facts (per serving): 35 Cal (1g fat, 0g protein, 3g fiber)

It's truly as if the Ukrainian menu is incomplete without this cucumber salad. It's made from cucumbers and green onions, which add lots of nutritional value to this salad.

Ingredients (4 servings)

3 cucumbers, peeled and sliced
½ teaspoon salt
½ cup green onions, chopped
1 tablespoon white vinegar
Dash white pepper
¼ cup sour cream

Preparation

Spread the cucumber in a colander and drizzle salt on top. Leave them for 15 minutes then transfer to a bowl. Add the black pepper, vinegar, onions, and sour cream. Finally, mix well. Serve.

Salad with Tongue and Bryndza

Preparation time: 10 minutes
Cook time: 3 hours
Nutrition facts (per serving): 155 Cal (8g fat, 13g protein, 2g fiber)

If you haven't tried this salad with tongue and Bryndza before, then here comes a simple and easy to cook recipe that you can recreate at home in no time with minimum efforts.

Ingredients (4 servings)
½ lb. beef tongue, diced
5 oz. Bryndza, soaked
2 boiled eggs, peeled and diced
1 bunch green lettuce
1 bunch green onions
1 red onion
3 fresh cucumbers
5 oz. mayonnaise
1 onion
Black pepper, to taste
5 pepper peas
Salt, to taste

Preparation
Cook the beef tongue in a pot filled with water to a boil. Stir in onions and cook for 3 hours on low heat. Drain and transfer to a bowl. Drain and dice the Bryndza and transfer to the tongue. Add the rest of the salad ingredients and mix well. Serve.

Garden Salad

Preparation time: 10 minutes
Nutrition facts (per serving): 212 Cal (16g fat, 5g protein, 4g fiber)

The colorful Ukrainian garden salad is super tempting in taste and looks. Serve at the table to increase your fiber intake.

Ingredients (4 servings)
10 large leaf romaine lettuce leaves, chopped
4 tomatoes, chopped
1 large cucumber, sliced
1 onion, sliced
½ cup fresh parsley, chopped
1 tablespoon salt
2 tablespoons lemon juice
1 tablespoon olive oil
1 cup sour cream

Preparation
Toss the tomatoes, romaine lettuce, onion, cucumber, and parsley in a large salad bowl. Whisk the lemon juice, olive oil, sour cream, and salt. Pour this cream mixture over the veggies and mix well. Serve.

Soups

Ukrainian Chicken Soup

Preparation time: 15 minutes
Cook time: 1 hour 31 minutes
Nutrition facts (per serving): 181 Cal (5g fat, 7g protein, 6g fiber)

If you haven't tried this Ukrainian chicken soup before, then here comes a simple and easy to cook recipe that you can recreate at home in no time with minimum efforts.

Ingredients (6 servings)

1 (3-lbs.) chicken, neck reserved
2 medium onions, chopped
2 carrots, scrubbed and diced
2 celery ribs, diced
1 large, unpeeled garlic clove, smashed
1 teaspoon whole black peppercorns
3 ½ quarts water
1 large fresh bay leaf
6 parsley sprigs
2 thyme sprigs
Salt, to taste
2 tablespoon unsalted butter
8 cups green cabbage, chopped
1 cup garlic dill pickles, sliced
¼ cup tomato paste
1 tablespoon sweet paprika
Freshly black pepper, to taste
½ cup reserved pickle juice
¼ cup chopped fresh dill
Sour cream, for garnish

Preparation

Add the chicken, thyme, parsley, bay leaf, peppercorns, garlic, celery, carrots, onion, water, and neck in a saucepan. Boil this mixture, reduce the heat, cover, and cook for 30 minutes on low heat. Transfer the prepared chicken to a plate and remove the chicken from the bones. Return the chicken bones to the cooking liquid and cook for 1 hour, then strain. Add 8 cups broth to a saucepan and cook for 30 minutes. Add the salt to season the broth. Sauté the onion, pickles, and cabbage with butter in a skillet for 10 minutes. Stir in the paprika and the tomato paste and cook for 1 minute. Stir in broth, black pepper, and salt. Next, cook for 20 minutes. Add the pickle juice, dill, and chicken. Serve warm.

Potato Egg Soup

Preparation time: 15 minutes
Cook time: 15 minutes
Nutrition facts (per serving): 121 Cal (3.9g fat, 4.8g protein, 2.8g fiber)

Yes, you can make something as delicious as this Okroshka by using only basic ingredients. Season the potatoes liberally for best taste.

Ingredients (8 servings)
8 cups cold water
⅓ cup sour cream
3 ½ tablespoon vinegar
2 ½ teaspoon salt
3 tablespoon dill, chopped
½ cup green onion, chopped
½ ham diced
3 medium cooked potatoes, peeled and diced
3 hard-boiled eggs, diced
3 cucumbers, diced

Preparation
Peel and dice the potatoes into ¼ inches cubes. Add potatoes to a pot and pour enough water to cover the potatoes. Add 1 tablespoon vinegar and boil the potatoes for 10 minutes. Drain and allow the potatoes to cool. Boil 3 eggs in boiling water, then transfer to an ice bath. Dice the eggs and transfer them to a cooking pot. Stir in cucumbers, ham, dill, green onions. Whisk 8 cups water, remaining vinegar, sour cream, and salt in a bowl. Pour this prepared mixture into the pot and cook for 5 minutes. Serve warm.

Bean Soup with Walnuts

Preparation time: 15 minutes

Cook time: 1 hour 40 minutes

Nutrition facts (per serving): 519 Cal (24g fat, 24g protein, 14g fiber)

Bean soup is always an easy way to add extra proteins and nutrients to your menu, and here some that you can make in just a few minutes.

Ingredients (6 servings)

2 ½ cups white beans

2 onions, diced

3 ½ oz. walnuts, chopped

1 tablespoon flour

3-oz. butter

Preparation

Add beans to cold water and soak for 12 hours. Drain and transfer the beans to a pot. Pour water into the beans and cook for 1 ½ hour on low heat until beans are soft. Mash one cup of beans and return it to the pan. Sauté onions in butter until soft. Add flour and mix well. Stir in thyme, coriander, and walnuts. Transfer this mixture to the beans and cook for 10 minutes. Serve warm.

Pea Soup

Preparation time: 15 minutes

Cook time: 1 hour 40 minutes

Nutrition facts (per serving): 109 Cal (4g fat, 9.5g protein, 3g fiber)

Here is a delicious and savory combination of smoked meat, peas, carrots, and bacon that you must add to your menu.

Ingredients (6 servings)

1 lb. smoked meat

1 ¼ cups peas

¼-lb. carrots roots

½ bunch spring onion

3 ½ oz. bacon pieces

Salt and black pepper, to taste

Preparation

Sauté onion, bacon pieces in a greased pan for 5 minutes. Transfer the mixture to a pot, then pour then peas and stir fry for 2 minutes. Pour in water to cover the peas and cook for 1 ½ hour. Adjust seasoning with salt and black pepper. Serve warm.

Ukrainian Red Borscht Soup

Preparation time: 15 minutes
Cook time: 25 minutes
Nutrition facts (per serving): 257 Cal (14g fat, 10g protein, 1g fiber)

The Ukrainian red borscht soup is a delight to serve at the dinner table. It's known for its unique pork mixed with potatoes flavors.

Ingredients (6 servings)

1 (16 oz.) package pork sausage
3 medium beets, peeled and shredded
3 carrots, peeled and shredded
3 medium baking potatoes, peeled and cubed
1 tablespoon vegetable oil
1 medium onion, chopped
1 (6 oz.) can tomato paste
¾ cup water
½ medium head cabbage, cored and shredded
1 (8 oz.) can diced tomatoes, drained
3 garlic cloves, minced
Salt and black pepper, to taste
1 teaspoon white sugar, or to taste
½ cup sour cream, for topping
1 tablespoon chopped fresh parsley for garnish

Preparation

Sauté the sausage in a skillet until golden brown. Add the sausage and water to a saucepan, cover, and cook to a boil. Stir in the beets and cook until their color changes. Stir in the potatoes and carrots and then cook for 15 minutes. Stir in the diced tomatoes and the cabbage. Sauté the onion with oil in a skillet until soft and then add the tomato paste. Mix well, then transfer to the pot, and then add garlic. Cover and leave for 5 minutes. Stir in the sugar, black pepper, and salt. Garnish with sour cream and parsley. Enjoy.

Ukrainian Cabbage Soup

Preparation time: 10 minutes
Cook time: 15 minutes
Nutrition facts (per serving): 350 Cal (17g fat, 31g protein, 1g fiber)

Try this Ukrainian cabbage soup with carrot with your favorite herbs on top. Adding a dollop of cream or yogurt will make it even richer in taste.

Ingredients (6 servings)

2 cup cabbage, shredded
7 sticks celery, chopped
6 carrots, chopped
5 garlic cloves
1 teaspoon black pepper
8 tablespoon olive oil
1 teaspoon oregano
1 leaf bay leaf
1 teaspoon celery salt
4 potatoes, chopped
4 onions, chopped
6 tomatoes, chopped
1 teaspoon salt
8 cups chicken broth
1 teaspoon spice thyme
1 teaspoon sage
1 teaspoon rosemary
1 teaspoon garlic salt

Preparation

Sauté the garlic and onions with oil in a soup pan until soft. Stir in the chicken broth and cook to a boil. Add the celery, carrots, and potatoes. Next, cook until the veggies are soft. Stir in the spices and the rest of the ingredients. Cook for 4 minutes, then serve warm.

Ukrainian Mushroom Soup

Preparation time: 10 minutes

Cook time: 30 minutes

Nutrition facts (per serving): 290 Cal (16g fat, 10.5g protein, 2g fiber)

Enjoy this mushroom soup with a fresh vegetable salad. You can adjust spices according to your taste preference and make a perfect entree for your dinner.

Ingredients (6 servings)

4 cups vegetable broth
2 medium potatoes diced
2 tablespoon olive oil
1 large onion finely minced
1 small carrot chopped
8 oz. Portobello mushrooms sliced
1 teaspoon thyme
1 cup half and half
3 garlic cloves
1 teaspoon salt
¼ teaspoon black pepper

Preparation

Sauté the onion and the carrot with 2 tablespoons oi in a suitable pan for 5 minutes. Stir in the mushrooms and the vegetables and then cook for 5 minutes. Stir in the stock and cook to a boil. Add the potatoes and cook for 15 minutes. Add the rest of the ingredients, cook for 5 minutes, and then blend with an immersion blender. Serve.

Vegetable Soup

Preparation time: 15 minutes

Cook time: 2 hours 10 minutes

Nutrition facts (per serving): 122 Cal (4g fat, 8g protein, 3g fiber)

This beef and root vegetable soup is a must to add to your Ukrainian menu because it has all the right ingredients to make your meal energy rich.

Ingredients (10 servings)

1-pound (453g) beef stew meat, diced

1 ½ teaspoons salt

¾ teaspoon pepper

7 cups of water

1 medium onion, chopped

1 tablespoon butter

8 cups cabbage, shredded

4 cups sliced carrots

2 celery ribs, sliced

2 medium potatoes, peeled and cubed

2 cups tomatoes, chopped

1 cup fresh beets, chopped

¼ cup fresh parsley, minced

1-½ tablespoons vinegar

2 tablespoons all-purpose flour

¾ cup half-and-half cream

Preparation

Fill a suitable pot with water and place it over high heat. Add the stew meat, black pepper, and salt. Cook the meat for 1 hour on a simmer. Set a small saucepan over medium heat. Add the butter and onion and then sauté until soft. Stir in the carrots, celery, tomatoes, potatoes, beets, cabbage, vinegar, and parsley. Next, boil. Reduce the heat and cook for 60 minutes on a simmer. Meanwhile, mix the flour with cream and add the mixture to the soup. Cook for 2 minutes until the soup thickens. Serve warm.

Ukrainian Beetroot Broth (Borsch)

Preparation time: 10 minutes
Cook time: 1 hour 47 minutes
Nutrition facts (per serving): 110 Cal (11g fat, 2g protein, 6g fiber)

Make this beetroot broth in no time and enjoy it with some garnish on top. Adding tomato salad on top makes it super tasty.

Ingredients (4 servings)
7 oz. beetroot, peeled and cut into matchsticks
7 oz. potatoes, peeled and chopped
2 tablespoon sunflower oil
1 onion, chopped
1 carrot, peeled and grated
1 red pepper, cored, deseeded and chopped
1 tablespoon tomato puree
1 beef tomato, peeled and grated
½ small white cabbage, shredded
1 -13 oz. can red kidney beans, drained and rinsed
Salt and black pepper, to taste

Preparation
Add the stock, water, bay leaf, onion, and meat to a saucepan and then cook for 1 hour on low heat. Stir in the potatoes and the beetroot, and then cook for 30 minutes. Stir in the black pepper and salt. Sauté the carrot and the onion with oil in a skillet for 7 minutes. Stir in the red pepper and the tomato puree, and then cook for 2 minutes. Stir in the grated tomato and return this mixture to the soup. Add the beans and the cabbage, and then cook for 7 minutes. Garnish with dill and sour cream. Serve.

Ukrainian Potato Soup

Preparation time: 15 minutes
Cook time: 10 minutes
Nutrition facts (per serving): 386 Cal (3g fat, 24g protein, 5g fiber)

If you're a potato lover enjoy nicely cooked potatoes in your soup, then here's a recipe that you can try. Enjoy it with your crispy bread.

Ingredients (4 servings)

2 tablespoon vegetable oil
1 onion chopped
1 ½ lb. potatoes diced
3 celery stalks diced
¼ green cabbage sliced into small pieces
8 cups chicken stock
1 cup sour cream
½ cup milk
2 tablespoon flour
Salt and pepper, to taste
¼ cup fresh dill

Preparation

Sauté the onion with 2 tablespoon of oil in the Instant Pot on Sauté mode. Stir in the rest of the vegetables and 8 cups water. Cover the pressure lid and cook on High pressure for 7 minutes. Allow the steam to release naturally for 10 minutes, then remove the lid. Blend the sour cream with 2 tablespoon flour and ½ cup milk in a blender. Add 2 cups vegetable mixture and blend again until smooth. Return this mixture to the pot along with black pepper, dill, and salt, and then serve warm.

Ukrainian Green Borsch (Sorrel Soup)

Preparation time: 15 minutes

Cook time: 40 minutes

Nutrition facts (per serving): 482 Cal (4g fat, 28g protein, 3g fiber)

If you haven't tried the green borsch before, then here comes a simple and easy to cook this recipe that you can recreate at home in no time with minimum efforts.

Ingredients (4 servings)

1 chicken back

5 potatoes, diced

1 carrot diced

1 beet diced

1 bell pepper diced

1 onion diced

10 ½ oz. sorrel

4 tablespoon vegetable oil

1 cup tomato juice

8 cups water

Salt, to taste

Black pepper, to taste

3 bay leaves

½ teaspoon paprika

3 cloves garlic, minced

Dill, to taste

Parsley, to taste

Green onion, to taste

Preparation

Add the chicken and 8 cups of water to a deep pan and cook to a boil. Reduce the heat and cook for 30 minutes. Add the vegetables to the chicken and cook until the potato is tender. Stir in the rest of the ingredients and continue cooking for 5 minutes. Serve warm.

Potato Pork Millet Soup (Kapustnyak Zaporizhian)

Preparation time: 15 minutes
Cook time: 30 minutes
Nutrition facts (per serving): 358 Cal (14g fat, 9g protein, 4g fiber)

You can give this potato pork millet soup a try because it has a good and delicious combination of vegetables and meat.

Ingredients (4 servings)
½ lb. pork
½ lb. sauerkraut
½ lb. potatoes
2 tablespoon millet
1 carrot
½ cup parsley
1 onion
3 tablespoon dairy butter
2 oz. salted pork fat
4 tablespoon sour cream
8 cups water
Salt, to taste
Black pepper, to taste
2 bay leaves

Preparation

Sauté the vegetables with pork fat in a deep pan for 5 minutes. Stir in the rest of the ingredients then continue cooking for 25 minutes. Puree half of this soup and return to the pot. Garnish with sour cream and parsley. Serve warm.

Chicken Solyanka Soup

Preparation time: 5 minutes

Cook time: 30 minutes

Nutrition facts (per serving): 470 Cal (28g fat, 36g protein, 1.7g fiber)

Try this chicken Solyanka soup for dinner. This warming bowl of soup is best to serve during winters at festive dinners and during special lunches.

Ingredients (4 servings)

Soup

2 large bay leaves

6 whole black peppercorns

4 whole allspice berries

10 cups water

4 tablespoon beef base

½ medium head green cabbage, shredded

1 cup coarsely chopped celery

1 tablespoon oil

2 medium onions, coarsely chopped

2 medium carrots, peeled and chopped

1 lb. dried Polish kabanosy sausage or any dry pork sausage, sliced

2 medium cooked chicken breasts, cubed

1 cup ham, cubed

3 large dill pickles, chopped

1 (6-oz.) can tomato paste

2 (14-oz.) cans stewed tomatoes

¾ cup sliced black olives

2 tablespoon capers

1 cup dry white wine

Salt, to taste

Freshly black pepper, to taste

Garnish

½ cup sour cream

½ cup fresh dill, chopped

Preparation

Tie the whole spices in a cheesecloth and place in a soup pot. Add the rest of the ingredients. Cook for 30 minutes on a simmer. Discard the tied spices. Serve warm.

Ukrainian Mushroom and Potato Soup

Preparation time: 10 minutes

Cook time: 30 minutes

Nutrition facts (per serving): 167 Cal (7.7g fat, 4.5g protein, 1g fiber)

The creamy mushroom and potato soup are the highlight of Ukrainian cuisine, and it's a must to add to your menu due to its rich nutritional content.

Ingredients (4 servings)

5 tablespoon butter

2 leeks, chopped

2 large carrots, sliced

6 cups chicken broth

2 teaspoon dried dill weed

2 teaspoon salt

⅛ teaspoon black pepper

1 bay leaf

2 lbs. potatoes, peeled and diced

1 lb. fresh mushrooms, sliced

1 cup half-and-half cream

¼ cup flour

1 sprig of fresh dill weed for garnish

Preparation

Add 3 tablespoon butter to a saucepan and melt over medium heat. Stir in the carrots and the leeks and sauté for 5 minutes. Pour in the broth, bay leaf, black pepper, and salt. Mix well and add the potatoes, then cook for 20 minutes. Meanwhile, sauté the mushrooms in the remaining butter for 5 minutes until golden brown. Add the mushrooms, flour, and half and half cream to the soup. Stir and cook the soup until the soup thickens. Serve warm.

Ukrainian Green Bean and Potato Soup

Preparation time: 10 minutes
Cook time: 30 minutes
Nutrition facts (per serving): 234 Cal (7.7g fat, 8.8g protein, 4g fiber)

Don't miss out on this green bean potato soup because a warming bowl p is everything that you need to complete your Ukrainian menu.

Ingredients (4 servings)
1 tablespoon vegetable oil
1 large onion, sliced
4 medium red potatoes, cubed
½ lb. green beans, chopped
5 cups vegetable broth
2 tablespoon whole wheat flour
½ cup sour cream
¾ cup sauerkraut with juice
1 tablespoon fresh dill, chopped
1 pinch salt and black pepper

Preparation
Place a large saucepan with vegetable oil over medium heat. Toss in the onion and sauté for 5 minutes. Stir in the green beans and the potatoes, then sauté for 5 minutes. Stir in the vegetable stock and cook to a boil, then cook for 15 minutes on a simmer. Stir in the sour cream and flour, and then cook until the soup thickens. Add dill, black pepper, salt, and dill, and then cook for 5 minutes. Serve warm.

Main Dishes

Cabbage Meat Stew

Preparation time: 15 minutes

Cook time: 1 hour 10 minutes

Nutrition facts (per serving): 336 Cal (2g fat, 33 protein, 12g fiber)

This cabbage meat stew is quite famous in the region; in fact, and it's a staple because of its nutritional content.

Ingredients (4 servings)

1 lb. bone-in meat, diced

2 tablespoon beef better than bullion

3 medium potatoes

½ small cabbage head

1 large carrot

1 small onion

10 oz canned diced tomatoes

Salt, to taste

Oil, to cook

Preparation

Sauté the onion and the carrots with oil in a soup pan for 5 minutes, add the meat, and sauté for 5 minutes. Stir in 4 quarts of water and cook for 30 minutes. Stir in the rest of the ingredients and then cook for 30 minutes. Serve warm.

Cabbage Pie

Preparation time: 15 minutes
Cook time: 1 hour 15 minutes
Nutrition facts (per serving): 141 Cal (11g fat, 4g protein, 0.5g fiber)

Stop waiting around and try this Ukrainian cabbage pie now! You'll be amazed at its crunchy texture and juicy taste.

Ingredients (8 servings)

3 tablespoon butter
1 small head cabbage, chopped
3 hard-boiled eggs, peeled and chopped
3 sprigs fresh dill, chopped
1 pinch salt
2 sheets puff pastry
1 egg, beaten

Preparation

Set a suitable skillet over medium-low heat and add butter to melt. Stir in cabbage and sauté for 30 minutes. Remove this hot pan from the heat and allow the cabbage to cool for 15 minutes. Meanwhile, set the oven at 400 degrees F to preheat. Transfer the cooked cabbage to a bowl and add dill, salt, and hard-boiled eggs. Mix well. Line a pie plate with puff pastry. Spread the prepared cabbage filling on top and cover with another puff pastry. Pinch the edges and brush the top with whisked eggs. Bake the pie for almost 45 minutes at 350 degrees F, then slice to serve.

Ukrainian Pork Roast

Preparation time: 15 minutes

Cook time: 2 hours

Nutrition facts (per serving): 273 Cal (11g fat, 36g protein, 2g fiber)

Do you want to enjoy a pork roast with a Ukrainian twist? Then try this Ukrainian Pork roast. You can serve this roast with boiled rice or with pasta.

Ingredients (6 servings)

2 ¼ lbs. bone-in pork loin chops

3 tomatoes, sliced

2 onions, sliced

¾ cup Gouda cheese, shredded

1 clove garlic, crushed

1 pinch salt and black pepper

3 tablespoon yellow mustard

Preparation

At 425 degrees F, preheat the oven. Carve ¼ inches cuts on top of the pork chops. Mix garlic with salt, black pepper, and mustard in a bowl. Add tomatoes, cheese, and onion to the slits and place the chops in a baking pan. Brush the chops with garlic mixture and cover the pan with aluminum foil, then bake for 1 hour 30 minutes. Uncover the chops and bake for 30 minutes more. Serve warm.

Beef Stroganoff

Preparation time: 15 minutes
Cook time: 1 hour 10 minutes
Nutrition facts (per serving): 303 Cal (23g fat, 17g protein, 2g fiber)

The classic beef stroganoff is here to complete your Ukrainian menu. This meal can be served on all special occasions and celebrations.

Ingredients (6 servings)

2 lbs. beef chuck roast, diced
½ teaspoon salt
½ teaspoon black pepper
4 oz. butter
4 green onions, sliced
4 tablespoon all-purpose flour
1 (10.5 oz.) can condensed beef broth
1 teaspoon mustard
1 (6 oz.) can sliced mushrooms, drained
⅓ cup sour cream
⅓ cup white wine
Salt, to taste
Black pepper, to taste

Preparation

Cut the roast into ½ inch thick slices. Rub the beef strips with black pepper and salt. Set a suitable skillet over medium heat and add butter to melt. Sear the beef strips for 5 minutes. Add flour to the beef juices and mix well. Pour in beef broth, then cook the mixture to a boil. Cover and reduce its heat to a simmer. Cook for 1 hour, then add sour cream, white wine and mushrooms. Adjust seasonings with black pepper and salt. Serve warm.

Stuffed Cabbage

Preparation time: 15 minutes
Cook time: 2 hours 30 minutes
Nutrition facts (per serving): 467 Cal (29g fat, 28g protein, 3g fiber)

The stuffed cabbage soaked in red sauce is an entrée that you must serve on the festive celebration. This recipe will add a lot of appeal and color to your dinner table.

Ingredients (10 servings)

1 head cabbage, cored

3 quarts water

¼ teaspoon salt

1 ½ lb. lean ground beef

1 ½ lb. ground pork

1 ½ cups white rice, cooked

¼ cup onion, finely chopped

2 tablespoon fresh parsley, chopped

2 large eggs, beaten

½ teaspoon garlic powder

½ teaspoon salt

½ teaspoon black pepper

1 (28 oz.) can tomato sauce

¼ cup white vinegar

2 ⅔ tablespoon white sugar

Preparation

Add water and ¼ teaspoon salt, to a stockpot and boil it. Add cabbage head to the boiling water and cook for 15 minutes while turning it after every 3 minutes. Remove the separate leaves from the pot. Drain and keep 12-oz. cabbage water aside. Leave the cabbage leaves in a colander. Mix beef with pork, rice, onion, egg, garlic powder, black pepper, salt, and parsley in a bowl. Place one cabbage leaves on a working surface. Add 2 teaspoon of the prepared beef mixture at the center of the leave. Roll the leaf and repeat the same with the remaining cabbage leaves and beef mixture. Place the prepared cabbage rolls in a casserole dish. Mix tomato sauce with white vinegar, white sugar, and water in a bowl. Pour this mixture over the cabbage rolls. Cover the prepared pan with aluminum foil and bake for 2 ½ hours in the oven at 350 degrees F.

Chicken Kiev

Preparation time: 15 minutes
Cook time: 20 minutes
Nutrition facts (per serving): 398 Cal (16g fat, 39g protein, 1.2g fiber)

The classic chicken Kiev is here to complete your Ukrainian menu. This meal can be served on all special occasions and celebrations.

Ingredients (6 servings)

⅓ cup butter
½ teaspoon black pepper
1 teaspoon garlic powder
2 lbs. boneless chicken breast, halves
2 large eggs
3 tablespoon water
¼ teaspoon black pepper
½ teaspoon garlic powder
1 teaspoon dried dill weed
¾ cup all-purpose flour
¾ cup dry breadcrumbs
2 cups vegetable oil for frying
½ lemon, sliced
¼ cup fresh parsley, chopped

Preparation

Mix 1 teaspoon garlic powder, ½ teaspoon black pepper, and ⅓ cup butter in a bowl. Line a baking pan with 6x6 inches aluminum foil.

Spread this butter mixture in the baking pan then freezes. Place the chicken on a working surface in between two wax papers. Pound the chicken with a mallet into ¼ inch thick. Remove the baking pan from the freezer. Cut the prepared butter into 6 pieces and place the butter piece on top of each chicken piece. Roll the chicken breast and secure the chicken roll with a toothpick. Beat eggs with water in a bowl. Mix flour, dill weed, ½ teaspoon garlic powder, and ¼ teaspoon black pepper in a bowl. Spread the breadcrumbs in a tray. Coat the chicken rolls with the flour mixture, dip in the eggs and then coat with the breadcrumbs. Place the coated chicken rolls in a shallow tray, then refrigerate for 30 minutes. Add vegetable oil to a suitable frying pan and heat up to 350 degrees F. Add chicken rolls and deep fry for 5 minutes per side until golden brown. Remove the chicken from the oil and garnish it with parsley. Serve warm.

Chicken Potato Stew

Preparation time: 10 minutes
Cook time: 28 minutes
Nutrition facts (per serving): 408 Cal (6.2g fat, 34g protein, 4g fiber)

The classic Ukrainian flavors are on the menu, and this time, you can add them through the chicken potato stew.

Ingredients (4 servings)

1 tablespoon butter
1¼ lb. boneless chicken breast, cubed
5 potatoes, peeled and cubed
1 carrot, sliced
1 onion, chopped
1 tablespoon tomato paste
1 pinch salt and black pepper
2 cups water to cover
1 bunch fresh parsley, chopped

Preparation

Set a large saucepan over medium heat. Add butter to melt then sear the chicken for 5 minutes per side. Stir in carrot, potatoes, and onion then sauté for 8 minutes. Add tomato paste, black pepper, and salt then add enough to water to cover the chicken. Cook for 15 minutes on a simmer. Garnish with parsley. Serve warm.

Verenike Casserole

Preparation time: 10 minutes
Cook time: 6 hours
Nutrition facts (per serving): 421 Cal (16g fat, 29g protein, 0g fiber)

Verenike, one of the fanciest casserole meals, is here to add flavors to your dinner table, this time with a mix of ham, milk, cheese, and cream.

Ingredients (8 servings)
1 (24 oz.) carton cottage cheese

3 large eggs, beaten

1 cup sour cream

2 cups evaporated milk

2 cups cooked ham, cubed

1 teaspoon salt

½ teaspoon black pepper

7 uncooked lasagna noodles

Preparation
Beat eggs with cottage cheese, evaporated milk, sour cream, salt, ham, and black pepper in a bowl. Add half of this mixture to a slow cooker. Spread noodles on top, then spread the other half of the cheese mixture. Cover and cook the casserole for 6 hours on low heat. Serve warm.

Kartoshnik with Cheese and Onions

Preparation time: 10 minutes
Cook time: 15 minutes
Nutrition facts (per serving): 271 Cal (19g fat, 9g protein, 3g fiber)

Let's have a rich and delicious combination of potatoes and cheese on a single platter with this Kartoshnik bake recipe. Try it now!

Ingredients (11 servings)

3 potatoes, peeled and quartered, boiled
5 eggs
¼ cup heavy whipping cream
¾ teaspoon salt
¾ cup sharp Cheddar cheese, shredded
¾ cup Swiss cheese, shredded
½ onion, chopped
3 teaspoon baking powder
½ cup butter, melted
1 ½ cup sour cream
½ cup green onions, chopped

Preparation

At 450 degrees F, preheat the oven. Grease a 9x9 inches baking dish with cooking oil. Beat eggs with salt and whipping cream in a bowl Stir in onions, cheese, and baking powder. Mash potatoes in another bowl. Add the potatoes (mashed) to the cream mixture. Mix well and spread the potato mash in a baking dish, then spread well. Bake the mashed potatoes for 5 minutes. Meanwhile, melt butter in a small pot. Cut the kartoshnik into 3x3 inches square and serve warm with melted butter, green onions, and sour cream on top. Enjoy.

Ukrainian Piroshki

Preparation time: 15 minutes
Cook time: 20 minutes
Nutrition facts (per serving): 184 Cal (4.7g fat, 20g protein, 1.7g fiber)

The Ukrainian Piroshki are famous for their earthy taste and refreshing aroma. Try them on your Ukrainian menu.

Ingredients (4 servings)

1 ½ cups 2 tablespoon vegetable oil
2 cups cabbage, sliced
½ cup onion, chopped
½ lb. ground beef
¾ teaspoon dried dill
½ teaspoon garlic powder
¾ teaspoon salt
¼ teaspoon black pepper
1 (16 oz.) package refrigerated biscuits

Preparation

Add 2 tablespoon oil to a suitable skillet and place it over medium heat. Stir in onion and cabbage, then sauté for 7 minutes. Transfer the prepared cabbage mixture to a bowl and keep it aside. Return the same skillet to medium-high heat. Stir in beef and sauté for 5 minutes until brown. Add sautéed cabbage and add black pepper, salt, garlic powder, and dill. Separate the biscuit in half to get 16 flat circles. Spread each circle into 3 inches rounds. Top each round with a tablespoon of meat mixture and fold the circles in half. Pinch the edges to seal the filling. Set a skillet over medium-high heat. Add 1 ½ cups oil to the skillet and heat to 350 degrees F. Fry the dumplings for almost 2 minutes per side until golden brown. Transfer the dumplings to a plate lined with a paper towel. Serve warm.

Ukrainian Chicken Stew

Preparation time: 15 minutes
Cook time: 75 minutes
Nutrition facts (per serving): 249 Cal (3.6g fat, 17g protein, 5.4g fiber)

It's about time to try some classic Ukrainian chicken stew on the menu and make it more diverse and flavorsome. Serve warm with warm bread.

Ingredients (4 servings)

2 lbs. boneless chicken thighs, diced

Chicken rub

1 teaspoon garlic powder
1 teaspoon onion powder
1 teaspoon poultry seasoning
1 teaspoon paprika
Salt and black pepper, to taste
1 large onion, diced
3 potatoes, peeled and diced
1 medium carrot, chopped
3 baby Bella mushrooms, diced
2 colorful small peppers, diced
3 bay leaves
1 ½ cup chicken broth
1 ½ teaspoon corn starch
2 tablespoon dill paste
Garlic powder, onion powder, paprika, poultry seasoning
Salt and black pepper, to taste
Olive oil

Preparation

Pat dry the chicken pieces and season them with onion powder, garlic powder, salt, black pepper, paprika and poultry seasoning. Sauté onion in a deep pan until brown. Transfer onion to a baking dish. Add chicken and more oil to a pan. Sear the prepared chicken for 5 minutes per side until golden brown. Stir in carrots and mushrooms, then cook for 5 minutes. Transfer this mixture to the baking dish. Add peppers and potatoes, then drizzle the remaining spice mixture on top of the chicken. Mix corn-starch with chicken broth in a saucepan and cook this mixture to a boil. Pour this mixture on top of the chicken and potatoes and drizzle bay leaves and dill on top. Cover the pan with a foil sheet, bake for 40 minutes at 350 degrees F. Uncover and bake for 20 minutes. Serve warm.

Ukrainian Shashlik

Preparation time: 10 minutes

Cook time: 15 minutes

Nutrition facts (per serving): 372 Cal (29g fat, 21g protein, 1.4g fiber)

Crispy and juicy Ukrainian shashliks are here to make your meal special. You can serve them with sautéed vegetables to complete the meal.

Ingredients (4 servings)

1 leg of boneless lamb, dice

1 yellow onion, diced

2 lemons, juiced

3 tablespoon olive oil

Fresh black pepper, to taste

2 teaspoons of salt

2 garlic cloves, minced

Preparation

Toss lamb meat with olive oil, black pepper, onion, salt, garlic, and lemon juice. Cover the marinate the meat for 4 hours in the refrigerator. Set the grill over high heat and grease its grilling grates. Thread the prepared meat on the skewers and grill each skewer for 6-7 minutes until meat is tender and golden brown in color. Drizzle black pepper and salt on top. Serve warm.

Mushroom Julienne

Preparation time: 15 minutes
Cook time: 25 minutes
Nutrition facts (per serving): 273 Cal (23g fat, 8g protein, 2g fiber)

This cheesy mushroom bake has a delicious and creamy sauce that tastes amazing when infused in nicely cooked mushrooms.

Ingredients (4 servings)

16 oz. white mushrooms, sliced

½ yellow onion, sliced

3 tablespoon butter

¼ cup white wine

¾ cup sour cream

½ cup heavy cream

Salt and black pepper, to taste

2 tablespoon mozzarella cheese, shredded

Preparation

At 375 degrees F, preheat the oven. Add mushrooms, onions, and 2 tablespoon butter to a pan. Sauté until mushrooms are soft. Transfer the mushrooms to a casserole dish. Set a small pot over medium heat. Add 1 tablespoon butter and white wine to a pot. Cook this mixture for 1 minute. Stir in sour cream and heavy cream. Add black pepper and salt. Boil this mixture and pour over the mushrooms. Drizzle cheese on top and bake for 10 minutes until melted.

Pork Solyanka

Preparation time: 15 minutes
Cook time: 13 minutes
Nutrition facts (per serving): 194 Cal (6g fat, 28g protein, 1.5g fiber)

If you are out of options, you can always cook the delicious pork Solyanka to surprise your family and loved ones.

Ingredients (6 servings)

8 cups bones stock
1 lb. smoked pork chops
2 onions, diced
2 pickled cucumbers
½ cup brine
2 tablespoon tomato paste
1 bay leaf
1 teaspoon black peppercorns
1 lemon
1 teaspoon oil or butter
1 fresh herb

Preparation

Add water and meat to a cooking pot and cook until the meat is soft. Strain the cooked broth and cut the meat into cubes. Add sliced cucumbers and tomato paste to a pan and cook for 3 minutes. Return the stock to a pot. Add tomato-cucumber mixture. Stir in onions, meat, bay leaf, and peppercorns. Cook the mixture for 10 minutes on a Simmer. Garnish with sour cream and herbs. Enjoy.

Grilled Trout

Preparation time: 15 minutes

Cook time: 15 minutes

Nutrition facts (per serving): 236 Cal (13.8g fat,18g protein, 1.7g fiber)

A perfect mix of fish with butter sauce, these trout fillets taste heavenly when baked and grilled in the grill.

Ingredients (2 servings)

2 trout, cut into fillets

1 tablespoon honey

1 tablespoon mustard

1 tablespoon vegetable oil

1 lemon

Black pepper and salt, to taste

Preparation

Clean and pat dry the trout. Mix mustard, honey, oil, honey, lemon juices, and lemon zest in a bowl. Rub the trout with black pepper and salt. Place the fillets in a baking tray. Drizzle the marinade on top and marinate for 10 minutes. Set a grill on medium-high heat and grease its grilling grates. Grill the fillets for 5 minutes per side until the fish is flaky and serve.

Cheese Fish

Preparation time: 15 minutes

Cook time: 10 minutes

Nutrition facts (per serving): 314 Cal (17g fat, 34g protein, 1g fiber)

The fish with cheese is famous for its unique taste and aroma, and now you can bring those exotic flavors home by using this recipe.

Ingredients (4 servings)

2 fillets cod fillets

5-oz. zucchini, peeled and diced

1 red bell pepper

7-oz. cheddar cheese, shredded

½ lemon

Black pepper and salt, to taste

Preparation

Rub the cod fillets with lemon juice. Place the prepared fillets in a baking tray lined with a foil sheet. Drizzle salt and black pepper on top. Spread zucchini, red bell pepper around the fillets. Add cheese on top. Roast the fish for 10 minutes at 350 degrees F. Serve warm.

Shashlik

Preparation time: 15 minutes
Cook time: 32 minutes
Nutrition facts (per serving): 286 Cal (11g fat, 28g protein, 3g fiber)

These pork shashliks are a must-have for every fancy dinner, and with the help of your grill, you can cook them in no time.

Ingredients (4 servings)
1 lb. lean pork
5 onions, finely chopped
4 cups kefir
Salt and black pepper, to taste

Preparation
Chop three onions and add them to a container. Toss in pork, salt, and black pepper. Mix well and cover to marinate for 24 hours in the refrigerator. Cut the remaining onions into slices. Thread the pork cubes and onion slices on the skewers. Set any grill over medium heat and grease its grilling grates with cooking oil. Grill the pork skewers for 8 minutes per side. Serve warm.

Chicken Shashlik

Preparation time: 15 minutes
Cook time: 24 minutes
Nutrition facts (per serving): 428 Cal (17g fat, 57g protein, 8g fiber)

The refreshing nut marinade always tastes great when used to marinate the delicious meals. In this recipe, you can serve it with cooked shashlik as well.

Ingredients (4 servings)

1-lb. chicken breast
1 bunch spring onions
2 garlic cloves, minced
½ lemon, juice
½ cup (50g) ground nuts
2 tablespoon olive oil
Salt and black pepper, to taste

Preparation

Mix green onion with ground nuts in a bowl. Stir in garlic and oil, then mix well. Rub the chicken cubes with black pepper and salt. Add chicken to the bowl and mix well. Cover and refrigerate for 30 minutes. Thread the chicken on the skewers. Set any grill over medium heat and grease its grilling grates. Grill the prepared skewers for 6 minutes per side until the chicken turns brown. Serve warm.

Lamb Shashlik

Preparation time: 15 minutes
Cook time: 24 minutes
Nutrition facts (per serving): 500 Cal (31g fat, 10g protein, 7g fiber)

Lamb shashliks are one option to go for in the meals. You can also keep them ready and stored, only to grill at the last minute.

Ingredients (6 servings)

1 ¼ lb. lamb, cut into cubes
⅔ cup dry white wine
4-oz. butter
⅙ lb. onions, diced
2 bunches of spring onion, chopped
⅔ lb. tomatoes, diced
⅔ lb. eggplant, diced
⅔ lb. bell pepper, diced
1 lemon
½ bunch parsley and dill
Salt and black pepper, to taste

Preparation

Add sugar, black pepper, and salt, to a bowl. Stir in wine and onions. Mix well and add meat to the marinade. Cover and refrigerate the meat for 3 hours. Slice the remaining onion and thread the lamb, veggies, and onion on the skewers alternately. Set the cooking grill on medium-high heat. Grill the prepared skewers for 6 minutes per side until golden brown. Drizzle melted butter and wine on top. Garnish with herbs and lemon juice. Serve warm.

Steamed Salmon

Preparation time: 15 minutes
Cook time: 20 minutes
Nutrition facts (per serving): 442 Cal (37g fat, 21g protein, 0g fiber)

Are in a mood to have a steamed salmon, well you can make it at home in just a few minutes using this quick recipe.

Ingredients (6 servings)

3 ⅓-lb. salmon
3 ½ oz. butter
1 cup dry white wine
½ cup pickle brine
1 bunch parsley, chopped
1 bay leaf

Sauce

1 bunch parsley
1 shallot, chopped
½ cup dry white wine
1 cup fish stock
7-oz. butter, cut into pieces
Salt and black pepper, to taste

Preparation

Add butter to a pan and place it over low heat Stir in pickle brine, white wine, bay leaf, and parsley. Cook this mixture to a boil, then add the salmon pieces. Cover and cook on low heat for 10 minutes. Meanwhile,

Sauté shallot in a pan with white wine. Pour in fish stock and cook this mixture until reduced to half. Remove this pan from the heat. Add black pepper, salt, and butter. Stir in parsley and cook until leaves are wilted. Top the salmon pieces with parley mixture. Serve warm.

Mushroom Caviar

Preparation time: 10 minutes
Cook time: 10 minutes
Nutrition facts (per serving): 295 Cal (28g fat, 3g protein, 2g fiber)

Have tried mushrooms cooked with a thick saucy based. Well, now you can enjoy this unique and flavorsome combination with this recipe.

Ingredients (2 servings)

4 ¼ oz. dried mushrooms
1 onion, chopped
4 tablespoon sunflower oil
2 garlic cloves, minced
2 tablespoon 5% vinegar
Salt and black pepper, to taste

Preparation

Soak mushrooms in cold water in suitable bowl for 3 hours then drain. Reserve the cooking liquid. Rinse and finely chop all the mushrooms. Now add the chopped mushrooms to the reserved cooking liquid. Cook the mushrooms until the liquid is completely evaporated. Sauté onions in a pan, then add mushrooms, garlic, vinegar, oil, black pepper, and salt for 10 minutes. Mix well and serve.

Ukrainian Pie

Preparation time: 15 minutes

Cook time: 30 minutes

Nutrition facts (per serving): 343 Cal (23g fat, 13g protein, 0.6g fiber)

Ukrainian Fish pies are always served as a complete meal, and this one, in particular, is great to have on a weight control diet.

Ingredients (6 servings)

2 teaspoon butter

1 (8 oz.) container sour cream

½ teaspoon baking soda

1 cup 3 tablespoon all-purpose flour

3 large eggs

½ cup mayonnaise

1 teaspoon salt

1 (6 ½ oz.) can salmon, drained and flaked

Preparation

At 400 degrees F, preheat the oven. Grease an iron skillet. Whisk sour cream with baking soda in a large bowl. Beat eggs in another bowl. Stir in 3 tablespoon flour, salt, and mayonnaise. Mix well until it makes a smooth and lump-free batter. Spread half of this batter on the greased pie plate. Add the fish on top of the batter and pour the remaining batter on top. Bake for 30 minutes in the preheated oven. Serve warm.

Ukrainian Chicken Pie

Preparation time: 10 minutes
Cook time: 30 minutes
Nutrition facts (per serving): 478 Cal (26g fat, 24g protein, 2g fiber)

These mini pies taste heavenly when they are cooked with chicken filling stuffed inside. Serve warm with your favorite dips.

Ingredients (8 servings)
Cream Cheese Pastry
4 oz. butter, diced
4 oz. cream cheese, diced
1 cup all-purpose flour

Chicken Pie Filling
1 cup of rice, cooked
2 large onions, sliced
8 oz. mushrooms, sliced
2 tablespoon butter
1 cup half-and-half cream
1 tablespoon cornstarch
1 cup chicken broth
3 cups cooked chicken meat, diced
2 tablespoon parsley, chopped
1 teaspoon salt
Black pepper, to taste
4 hard-cooked eggs, chopped
1 tablespoon dill, chopped

Egg Wash

1 egg yolk

1 tablespoon water

Preparation

Whisk all the ingredients for the dough to a food processor and process the dough for 20 seconds. Cover and refrigerate the dough until the filling is ready. Set a suitable skillet over medium heat and add 2 tablespoon butter to melt. Stir in mushrooms and onion, then sauté until caramelized. Mix half and half and cornstarch in a bowl and add to the onion. Mix well and add 1 cup chicken broth. Cook the mixture to a boil, then reduce its heat to a simmer. Cook for 1 minute, then add salt, black pepper, parsley, and chicken. Remove this pan from the heat and heat. Mix eggs with dill in a bowl. At 400 degrees F, preheat the oven. Spread ⅓ cooked rice at the bottom of a greased pan, then top this layer with ½ of the chicken mixture and then layer the ½ of the egg-dill mixture on top. Repeat these layers with a layer of remaining rice on top. Spread the pastry crust on top and brush it with egg wash. Bake the pie for 30 minutes until it bubbles. Serve warm.

Ukrainian Lamb Rice

Preparation time: 15 minutes
Cook time: 1 hour 35 minutes
Nutrition facts (per serving): 338 Cal (10g fat, 33g protein, 3g fiber)

Now you can quickly make flavorsome lamb and serve them to have a fancy meal for yourself and your guest.

Ingredients (4 servings)

2 oz. raisins
4 oz. pitted prunes
1 tablespoon fresh lemon juice
1-oz. butter
1 large onion, chopped
1 lb. boneless lamb, diced
8 oz. lean ground lamb
2 garlic cloves, crushed
2 ½ cups lamb stock
2 cups white rice, rinsed and drained
1 pinch saffron
Salt and black pepper, to taste
Parsley, for garnish

Preparation

Add prunes and raisins to a bowl and pour water and lemon juice to soak them for 1 hour. Drain and chop the prunes. Set a suitable pan over medium heat, add butter and sauté for 5 minutes. Stir in ground lamb, cubes of lamb, and garlic cloves. Sauté for 5 minutes until brown. Add

⅔ cup stock to the pan and cook this mixture to a boil, then reduce its heat. Cover and cook the mixture on a simmer for 1 hour. Pour in remaining stock and boil. Add white rice and saffron. Cook for 15 minutes on a simmer. Add prunes, black pepper, salt, and drained raisins. Cook for 5 minutes. Garnish with parsley. Serve warm.

Potato Turnip Stew

Preparation time: 10 minutes
Cook time: 35 minutes
Nutrition facts (per serving): 321 Cal (10g fat, 6.5g protein, 10g fiber)

Spicy and saucy Ragu is always a delight on a menu. Now you can make it easily at home by using the following simple ingredients.

Ingredients (4 servings)
1 tablespoon sunflower oil
1 large onion, chopped
4 carrots, peeled and diced
2 large red potatoes, peeled and diced
1 medium rutabaga, peeled and diced
1 medium turnip, peeled and diced
1 parsnip, peeled and diced
1 medium celeriac, peeled and diced
1 cup vegetable stock
½ cup parsley, chopped
2 tablespoon butter

Preparation
Add onion and oil to a large skillet and sauté for 5 minutes. Stir in celeriac, parsnip, turnip, rutabaga, potatoes, and carrots, then sauté for 10 minutes. Pour in the vegetable stock and cook the mixture for 20 minutes on a simmer. Stir in butter and parsley. Adjust seasoning with black pepper and salt. Serve warm.

Ukrainian Kotletki

Preparation time: 10 minutes

Cook time: 15 minutes

Nutrition facts (per serving): 478 Cal (11g fat, 55g protein, 3g fiber)

Enjoy this delicious mix of beef with spices and veggies. It is one nutritious mix of all your favorite ingredients.

Ingredients (4 servings)

2 slices white bread

½ cup milk

1 medium onion, peeled and grated

12 oz. pork ground

12 oz. ground beef

1 ½ teaspoon salt

½ teaspoon black pepper

1 ½ cups breadcrumbs

1 cup vegetable oil for frying

Preparation

Soak the bread in milk and then transfer it to a large bowl. Stir in meats, salt, black pepper, and onion. Mix well and make golf-ball sized meatballs out of this mixture. Press the meatballs into cutlets. Coat the cutlets with breadcrumbs and leave them for 10 minutes in a large skillet; heat oil for deep frying. Add the cutlets to the oil and cook for 5 minutes per side until golden brown. Serve warm.

Pork Loin Steaks

Preparation time: 10 minutes
Cook time: 25 minutes
Nutrition facts (per serving): 391 Cal (27g fat, 27g protein, 2g fiber)

Try seasoning the pork meat with seasoning, cook it with the stroganoff sauce and discover a whole new realm of flavors.

Ingredients (4 servings)

4 boneless loin steaks
Salt and black pepper, to taste
2 tablespoon butter
½ cup sweet onion, diced
3 garlic cloves, finely minced
2 tablespoon butter
1 lb. white button mushrooms, quartered
¼ cup red wine
1 tablespoon Worcestershire sauce
1 tablespoon red pepper jelly
2 teaspoon prepared yellow mustard
½ teaspoon salt
¼ cup heavy cream
¼ cup sour cream

Preparation

Pound the pork loin steaks with a mallet into a 1-inch thickness. Rub both sides of the steaks with black pepper and salt. Set a skillet over medium heat and 2 tablespoon Butter to heat. Sear the pork steaks for

5 minutes per side. Transfer the cooked pork to a plate and add more butter, onion, and garlic to the same pan. Sauté for 1 minute. Stir in mushrooms and butter. Sauté until the mushroom's liquid is released. Stir in red pepper jelly, mustard, Worcestershire sauce, and wine. Return the cooked pork to the pan, cover, and cook the pork for 5 minutes on a simmer. Transfer the pork to the serving plate. Add cream and ½ teaspoon salt, to the mushrooms in the pan. Cook the mixture until it thickens. Pour the prepared sauce on top of the pork and serve warm.

Ukrainian Chicken Rice

Preparation time: 10 minutes
Cook time: 45 minutes
Nutrition facts (per serving): 596 Cal (17g fat, 67g protein, 4g fiber)

Chicken Plov is loved by all, the old and the young, and they make a healthy meal. Try this recipe to make some.

Ingredients (6 servings)

3 lbs. chicken breast, boneless
3 cups of enriched parboiled rice
2 large onions, chopped
8 large carrots, chopped
3 heads of garlic, top removed
2 tablespoon cumin
1 tablespoon black peppercorns
Salt, to taste
Vegetable oil, for frying

Preparation

Add olive oil to a heavy-bottomed pan and place it over medium heat. Add meat and sauté until brown. Add black pepper and salt, then add onions and carrots. Continue to cook for 15 minutes with occasional stirring. Add enough water to cover this mixture and cook it to a boil. Stir in cumin, garlic, black peppercorns, and salt. Add chicken and rice to the pot and cook for 30 minutes. Serve warm.

Turkey Kotleti

Preparation time: 10 minutes

Cook time: 20 minutes

Nutrition facts (per serving): 292 Cal (13g fat, 41g protein, 0.5g fiber)

If you want your turkey and pork Kotleti to be extra crispy on the outside and super juicy and tasty on the inside, then give this quick recipe a try.

Ingredients (6 servings)

1 lb. ground pork

1 lb. ground turkey

1 onion, grated

½ cup white breadcrumbs

1 egg

2 tablespoon parsley, chopped

½ teaspoon salt

½ teaspoon garlic powder

¼ teaspoon black pepper

1 tablespoon mayo

Olive oil, to cook

Preparation

Add pork, turkey, onion, egg, parsley, salt, garlic powder, ground pepper, and mayo to a bowl. Mix well and make golf-ball sized meatballs out of this mixture. Press the meatballs into cutlets. Coat the cutlets with breadcrumbs and leave them for 10 minutes. In a large skillet, heat oil for deep frying. Add the cutlets to the oil and cook for 5 minutes per side until golden brown. Serve warm.

Chicken Kotleti

Preparation time: 10 minutes

Cook time: 20 minutes

Nutrition facts (per serving): 308 Cal (10g fat, 44g protein, 0.4g fiber)

If you want something exotic on your dinner table, then nothing can taste better this spiced chicken and pork Kotleti.

Ingredients (6 servings)

1-lb. ground pork

1-lb. ground chicken

1 egg

1 tablespoon mayo

1 onion, grated

½ teaspoon salt

¼ teaspoon black pepper

½ cup Italian breadcrumbs

Coating

1 ½ cups Italian breadcrumbs

Preparation

Add pork, chicken, egg, mayo, onion, salt, ½ cup breadcrumbs, and black pepper. Mix well and make golf-ball sized meatballs out of this mixture. Press the meatballs into cutlets. Coat the cutlets with breadcrumbs and leave them for 10 minutes, in a large skillet; heat oil for deep frying. Add the cutlets to the oil and cook for 5 minutes per side until golden brown. Serve warm.

Chicken Cabbage Pirog

Preparation time: 10 minutes
Cook time: 25 minutes
Nutrition facts (per serving): 557 Cal (19g fat, 33g protein, 5g fiber)

Chicken Pirog is one way to complete your Ukrainian menu; here is a recipe that you can try to have a delicious meal.

Ingredients (4 servings)
Dough
2 tablespoon mayonnaise

1 teaspoon oil

1 teaspoon salt

⅓ cup warm milk

⅓ cup warm water

1 ½ teaspoon active dry yeast

1 ½ teaspoon granulated sugar

2 cups all-purpose flour sifted

Filling
¾ lb. chicken breast, boneless, cubed

1 teaspoon oil

½ large onion, chopped

3 tablespoon butter

3 cups cabbage, shredded

2 small carrots, grated

2 garlic cloves, minced

¼ cup water

1 ½ teaspoon ketchup

1 ½ teaspoon sour cream

3 tablespoon herbs

1 egg with 1 teaspoon water beaten

½ teaspoon sesame seeds

Preparation

Prepare the dough by mixing mayo, salt, water, milk, oil, and yeast in a bowl. Cover and leave it for 5 minutes. Stir in flour and mix until it makes a smooth dough. Knead well and cover the dough for 2 hours at a warm place in the kitchen. Meanwhile, set a skillet over medium-high heat. Add chicken with 1 teaspoon oil to the pan and sauté for 3 minutes. Remove the chicken from the skillet. Add onion and 1 tablespoon butter and sauté until soft. Stir in cabbage, 2 tablespoon butter, garlic, water, carrots, cabbage, black pepper, and salt. Sauté until the cabbage is soft. Stir in sour cream, herbs, ketchup, and chicken to the pan. Cover and cook for 1 minute. Remove this filling from the heat and allow it to cool. Divide the dough into 2 parts and spread each into 12 inches round. Divide the cabbage on top of each dough round and fold the edges of dough then pinch the edges. Set the Pirog in a baking sheet, brush both the Pirog with egg wash and drizzle sesame seeds. Let them rise in 45 minutes. Bake for almost 22 minutes at 400 degrees F until golden brown.

Clam Stew

Preparation time: 10 minutes
Cook time: 30 minutes
Nutrition facts (per serving): 324 Cal (16g fat, 13g protein, 3g fiber)

Let's make quick clam chowder with these simple ingredients. Mix them together, then cook to have great flavors.

Ingredients (6 servings)

6 lean bacon slices, cut into ½" strips
2 carrots, sliced
2 celery ribs, diced
1 small onion, diced
4 tablespoon all-purpose flour
2 cups chicken broth
1 cup clams with their juice, chopped
1 bay leaf
1 ½ teaspoon Worcestershire sauce
½ teaspoon Tabasco sauce
½ teaspoon dried thyme
1 ½ teaspoon salt
¼ teaspoon black pepper
6 medium potatoes, peeled
2 cups of milk
1 cup whipping cream

Preparation

Place a suitable Dutch oven over medium heat and add bacon to sauté until crispy. Transfer this bacon to a plate. Add the celery, onion, and carrots to the pan and sauté for 8 minutes. Stir in 4 tablespoons of flour, and then mix well for 1 minute. Add the chicken broth, clams, bay leaf, and all other ingredients. Cook the soup for 20 minutes. Serve warm.

Buckwheat Mushroom Croquettes

Preparation time: 10 minutes
Cook time: 20 minutes
Nutrition facts (per serving): 259 Cal (5 g fat, 13g protein, 6g fiber)

Count on these buckwheat croquettes to make your dinner extra special and surprise your loved one with the ultimate flavors.

Ingredients (4 servings)
1 cup buckwheat groats, cooked
½-lb. white button mushrooms, sliced
1 medium onion, diced
1 medium carrot, grated
2 large eggs
1 tablespoon semolina flour
Salt and black pepper, to taste
¾ cup plain bread crumbs
Olive oil, to sauté

Preparation
Boil the buckwheat in salted water in a cooking pot. Drain and grind the cooked buckwheat in a food processor. Sauté the onion and carrot with 2 tablespoon oil in a suitable skillet over medium heat for 5 minutes. Stir in mushrooms and sauté for 5 minutes. Transfer the veggies to the buckwheat and mix well. Whisk 1 egg with the semolina, black pepper, and salt, to the buckwheat. Mix well and make small patties from this mixture. Beat the other egg in a small bowl. Dip the buckwheat croquettes in the egg and coat them with breadcrumbs. Add olive oil to a cooking pot and cook the croquettes for 3 minutes per side until golden brown. Serve warm.

Fish Ukha

Preparation time: 10 minutes
Cook time: 40 minutes
Nutrition facts (per serving): 382 Cal (13g fat, 19g protein, 6g fiber)

This fish soup will melt your heart away with its epic flavors. This soup has a juicy mix of veggies, fish, and spices that you easy to get and cook.

Ingredients (6 servings)

7 small fishes, skinless
4 onions, chopped
2 carrots, chopped
4 potatoes, diced
2 heads of Garlic, peeled and minced
2 celeries, chopped
1 bell pepper, chopped
1 bay leaf
Salt, to taste

Preparation

Wash all vegetables and fish in cold water. Drop the fish into a metal pot, fill it with water, and bring it to boil. Add 3 onions, carrots, garlic, salt, and pepper, and allow the broth to simmer for at least 30 minutes. Peel and cut all the potatoes into small pieces. Remove the onions, garlic, and fish from the pan. Add the potatoes and cook until soft. Add some pieces of fish and fry the remaining onion in some butter. Add the onions into the soup. Simmer for 10 minutes. Serve.

Chicken and Beef Croquettes

Preparation time: 10 minutes
Cook time: 15 minutes
Nutrition facts (per serving): 381 Cal (17g fat, 47g protein, 1g fiber)

These croquettes are one option for memorable meals. You can also keep them ready and stored, only to cook at the last minute.

Ingredients (6 servings)
3 slices whole-wheat bread, crusts removed
⅓ cup whole milk
1-lb. ground chicken
1-lb. lean ground beef
⅓ cup onion, finely diced
3 tablespoon unsalted butter, melted
2 eggs, separated into yolks and whites
2 tablespoon fresh dill, chopped
½ tablespoon salt
½ teaspoon black pepper

Breading
2 eggs, beaten
1 cup dry Italian breadcrumbs
Olive Oil and unsalted butter, to sauté

Preparation
Soak the bread in milk in a suitable bowl for 5 minutes, then transfer to a mixing bowl. Stir in the chicken, beef, onion, butter, eggs, dill, salt,

and black pepper, and then mix well. Make small patties from this mixture. Beat the eggs for breading in a bowl. Dip the prepared croquettes in the eggs and coat them with the breadcrumbs. Add the olive oil to a cooking pot and sear the croquettes for 5 minutes per side until golden brown. Serve warm.

Turkey Kotleti with Mushroom Filling

Preparation time: 15 minutes
Cook time: 23 minutes
Nutrition facts (per serving): 212 Cal (9g fat, 27g protein, 0.5g fiber)

These seasoned and stuffed Kotleti are irresistible. Try them with any of your favorite sauce.

Ingredients (6 servings)
1 lb. lean ground turkey
½ lb. (225g) lean ground beef
½ large onion, grated
1 garlic clove, grated
½ medium zucchini, grated
1 large egg
1 teaspoon salt
⅛ teaspoon black pepper, ground
1 tablespoon mayo
1 tablespoon flour
Oil, to sauté

Mushroom and buckwheat filling
¼ large onion, chopped
½-lb. mushrooms, sliced
1 cup cooked buckwheat
Salt, to taste

Preparation

Set a large pan with 1 tablespoon oil over medium heat. Toss in the onion and sauté for 2 minutes until soft. Stir in the mushrooms and sauté for 5 minutes. Add the buckwheat and salt. sauté for 1 minute, then remove this pan from the heat. Mix all the ingredients for the patties in a bowl. Make small patties from this mixture. Press each patty and top it with 1 teaspoon mushroom filling. Cover this filling with the patty mixture and seal well. Coat the patties with flour. Add oil to a pan and heat to 350 degrees F. Sear the stuffed patties for 5 minutes per side until golden brown. Serve warm.

Potatoes in A Garlic Cream Sauce

Preparation time: 10 minutes

Cook time: 23 minutes

Nutrition facts (per serving): 270 Cal (12g fat, 4g protein,6 g fiber)

These garlic potatoes have unique flavors due to their creamy seasoning. Keep this seasoning ready in your kitchen to enjoy this mix whenever you want.

Ingredients (4 servings)

2 lbs. new potatoes, quartered

½ tablespoon of sea salt

1 tablespoon olive oil

½ onion, diced

1 garlic clove, pressed

¾ cup heavy whipping cream

¼ cup fresh dill, chopped

Preparation

Add the potatoes, salt, and water to a saucepan and cook for 20 minutes, then drain. Set a skillet with a tablespoon olive over medium heat and add garlic and sauté for 1 minute. Stir in the salt and whipping cream, then boil for 2 minutes. Stir in the dill and potatoes, and then mix well. Cook for 5 minutes. Enjoy.

Chicken Butter Kiev

Preparation time: 15 minutes

Cook time: 20 minutes

Nutrition facts (per serving): 456 Cal (31g fat, 26g protein, 0.7g fiber)

The chicken with butter filling tastes great. Plus, it offers an interesting combination with the butter sauce.

Ingredients (4 servings)

Chicken Kiev

4 Chicken Breasts

2 eggs, beaten

¾ cup flour

1 ½ cups white breadcrumbs

Salt and black pepper, to taste

Olive oil or Canola oil to sauté

Kiev Butter

8 tablespoon unsalted Butter

1 garlic clove, minced

1 tablespoon lemon juice

2 tablespoon fresh parsley, chopped

½ teaspoon salt

½ teaspoon black pepper

Preparation

Prepare the Kiev butter and mix the butter, garlic, lemon juice, parsley, black pepper, and salt in a bowl. Wrap the prepared butter in plastic wrap and freeze for 30 minutes. Place the chicken breast in between two plastic sheets. Pound the chicken with a mallet into ¼ inch thickness. Top each chicken breast with ¼ of the Kiev butter and roll the chicken breasts. Beat the eggs in a bowl, mix the flour with black pepper and salt on a plate, and spread the breadcrumbs in a bowl. Coat the rolled chicken breasts in the flour, dip in the eggs and coat with the breadcrumbs. Add oil to a suitable pan and heat over medium heat. Sear the chicken Kiev for 2 minutes per side until golden brown. Place the Kievon a baking sheet and bake for 18 minutes in the oven at 350 degrees F in an oven. Serve warm.

Stuffed Cabbage Rolls (Golubtsi)

Preparation time: 15 minutes
Cook time: 25 minutes
Nutrition facts (per serving): 509 Cal (14g fat, 39g protein, 7g fiber)

Golubtsi is one option for dinner. You can also keep them ready and stored, only to assemble at the last minute.

Ingredients (8 servings)
6 cups cooked white rice
2 medium cabbages
1-lb. ground pork
1-lb. ground turkey
2 large eggs
6 medium carrots, grated
2 cups mushroom marinara sauce
¼ cup white vinegar
Olive oil
1 tablespoon butter
1 tablespoon sour cream
1 teaspoon Mrs. dash
Salt, to taste

Preparation
Mix the pork, turkey, eggs, rice, and white vinegar in a bowl. Whisk the butter with sour cream, dash, and salt in another bowl. Boil the cabbages in salted water until leaves are soft. Separate the leaves and spread them on a working surface. Divide the pork mixture on top of

each leaf and fold to wrap the filling. Place the prepared cabbage rolls in a baking pan. Pour the sauce on top and add a dollop of cream on top of each roll. Bake them for about 25 minutes at 450 degrees F in the oven. Serve warm.

Chicken Tenders

Preparation time: 15 minutes
Cook time: 20 minutes
Nutrition facts (per serving): 346 Cal (9.9g fat, 59g protein, 0.1g fiber)

Chicken cutlets are our favorite go-to meal when it comes to serving; these cutlets are easy to prepare in a no time.

Ingredients (4 servings)
2 lbs. (1kg) boneless skinless chicken tenders
Salt and black pepper, to taste
Canola oil, for sautéing

Egg wash
2 large whole eggs
1 tablespoon mayonnaise
1 tablespoon all-purpose flour
3 tablespoon milk
½ teaspoon Mrs. Dash seasoning
⅛ teaspoon salt

Breading
2 cups Italian breadcrumbs
3 tablespoon flour

Preparation

Prepare the egg wash and whisk the eggs with mayonnaise and milk. Mix the flour with the Mrs. Dash seasoning and salt in a shallow bowl. Spread the breadcrumbs on another plate. Pound the chicken tenders with a mallet into ¼ inches thickness. Rub the chicken with black pepper and salt. Add the canola oil to a deep pan and heat for deep frying. Coat the chicken with flour mixture, dip in the eggs and coat with breadcrumbs. Sear the chicken in the hot until golden brown. Serve.

Trout with Parsley Butter

Preparation time: 10 minutes
Cook time: 10 minutes
Nutrition facts (per serving): 268 Cal (26g fat, 9g protein, 0.3g fiber)

Trout with butter is served the most in the Ukrainian culinary tradition. Now you can also make this rich trout recipe.

Ingredients (2 servings)
1 large trout, cut into fillets
4 tablespoon unsalted butter softened
2 tablespoon lemon juice
3 tablespoon fresh parsley, chopped
Salt and black pepper, to taste

Preparation
Mix the butter with the lemon juice, parsley, salt, and ground pepper in a bowl. Place the trout on a baking sheet and pour half of the garlic mixture over the fish. Bake the fish for almost 10 minutes in the oven at 325 degrees F. Serve warm with the remaining garlic butter.

Pork Tefteli In A Cream Sauce

Preparation time: 5 minutes

Cook time: 20 minutes

Nutrition facts (per serving): 506 Cal (10g fat, 51g protein, 48g fiber)

These meatballs will make your day with the delightful taste and the special sauce that's poured on top before serving.

Ingredients (6 servings)

1 lb. ground pork

1 lb. ground chicken

2 cups cooked white rice

1 large egg

2 large garlic cloves

½ onion, grated

½ teaspoon salt

¼ teaspoon black pepper

2 slices of soft white bread

¾ cup milk

2 cups Italian Style Breadcrumbs

Tefteli Sauce

2 tablespoon olive oil

½ onion, chopped

1 large carrot, grated

2 tablespoon flour

1 tablespoon sour cream

1 cup heavy whipping cream

1 cup chicken broth

1 teaspoon paprika

Salt and black pepper, to taste

Canola oil or grapeseed oil

Preparation

Soak the bread in milk for 5 minutes, then transfer to a bowl. Add the pork, chicken and all other ingredients to the bowl. Mix well and make 1-inch balls from this mixture. Roll the balls in the breadcrumbs. Set a skillet with ¼ cup oil over medium heat. Sear the balls for 4 minutes per side. Serve these balls with Tefteli gravy on top. Set a saucepan over medium heat and add 2 tablespoon olive oil, carrot, onion, and then sauce until soft. Stir in the sour cream and flour, and then mix well until evenly incorporated. Stir in the broth, paprika, heavy cream, black pepper, and salt. Mix well and cook until it boils.

Potatoes with Pork

Preparation time: 15 minutes
Cook time: 50 minutes
Nutrition facts (per serving): 249 Cal (7g fat, 21g protein, 3g fiber)

If you want something new flavors in your meals, then this recipe is best to bring variety to the menu!

Ingredients (6 servings)

5 cups russet potatoes, peeled and cubed
½ teaspoon salt
⅛ teaspoon black pepper
½ teaspoon Mrs. Dash
2 tablespoon dill fresh

Onion mix

1 onion, chopped
2 medium carrots, grated
1 ½ tablespoon canola oil

Meat

1 lb. pork sirloin chops, boneless, diced
2 large garlic cloves pressed
½ teaspoon salt
⅛ teaspoon black pepper
1 ½ tablespoon canola oil
3 tablespoon tomato sauce
2 oz. jar pimiento peppers, diced and drained
2 ½ cups water

Preparation

Mix the pork cubes with garlic cloves, black pepper, and salt in a bowl, then cover. Refrigerate for 30 minutes to marinate. Meanwhile, heat the canola oil in a pan and add carrots, and onions then sauté until soft. Add the potatoes, salt, black pepper, and Mrs. Dash, then sauté for 5 minutes. Add 1 ½ tablespoon canola oil to a Dutch oven and place it over medium heat. Add the marinated pork to the oil and sear for 5 minutes per side. Add the tomato sauce, pimiento, and veggies mixture. Then pour in water and cook for 35 minutes. Serve warm.

Desserts

Ukrainian Apple Cake (Yabluchnyk)

Preparation time: 10 minutes
Cook time: 50 minutes
Nutrition facts (per serving): 167 Cal (8g fat, 7g protein, 3g fiber)

This apple cake is everything I was looking for. The mildly sweet apple flavor infused cake tastes great when prepared using the following combination of ingredients.

Ingredients (6 servings)
Cake
4 apples
1 ½ cups all-purpose flour
¼ cup sugar
¼ teaspoon salt
2 teaspoon baking powder
½ cup butter
1 egg
⅓ cup cream

Streusel topping
2 tablespoon butter
½ cup brown sugar
2 tablespoon all-purpose flour
2 teaspoon cinnamon

Preparation

At 375 degrees F, preheat your oven. Layer a 9-inch cake pan with parchment paper and grease with cooking oil. Mix the egg with the cream and the rest of the cake ingredients, except apples. Next, mix well until it makes soft dough. Spread this dough in the cake pan and arrange the apples on top. Mix all the streusel ingredients in a bowl and spread over the cake, and serve. Bake the cake for 40-50 minutes in the oven until golden brown. Slice and serve.

Ukrainian Honey Babka

Preparation time: 10 minutes
Cook time: 32 minutes
Nutrition facts (per serving): 185 Cal (8g fat, 2.9g protein, 3g fiber)

The Ukrainian honey babka is loved by all, the old and the young, and it makes a healthy dessert due to the mix of honey with sour cream, flour, etc.

Ingredients (6 servings)
Babka
2 ½ cups all-purpose flour
8 eggs
1 cup granulated sugar
1 cup honey, microwaved
16 oz. sour cream
2 teaspoon baking soda
2 tablespoon white distilled vinegar
½ teaspoon fine salt

Frosting
8 oz. cream cheese
8 oz. cool whip
½ cup powdered sugar

Preparation
At 350 degrees F, preheat your oven. Layer an 11x17 inch baking sheet with parchment paper. Beat the eggs with the rest of the babka

ingredients in a bowl until it makes a smooth batter. Spread this batter on the baking sheet and bake for 32 minutes. Allow the babka to cool and then cut into squares. Prepare the frosting ingredients in a bowl and add on top of the babka squares using a piping bag. Serve.

Ukrainian Honey Cake

Preparation time: 10 minutes

Cook time: 20 minutes

Nutrition facts (per serving): 379 Cal (11g fat, 34g protein, 3g fiber)

If you haven't tried the honey cake before, then here comes a simple and easy to cook recipe that you can recreate at home in no time with minimum efforts.

Ingredients (6 servings)

1 cup honey, warmed

4 eggs, beaten

1 ½ cups flour

1 teaspoon baking powder

Preparation

At 375 degrees F, preheat your oven. Dust a 7 inches cake pan with flour. Beat the honey and the egg in a bowl. Stir in the flour and the baking powder, and then mix well. Spread the dough in the prepared pan and bake for 20 minutes in the oven. Allow the cake to cool and serve.

Ukrainian Sweet Cheese

Preparation time: 15 minutes

Cook time: 60 minutes

Nutrition facts (per serving): 188 Cal (0.1g fat, 0.5g protein, 2g fiber)

If you want some new flavors on your dessert menu, then this sweet cheese recipe is best to bring variety to the menu.

Ingredients (6 servings)

2 lbs. cottage cheese

1 cup granulated sugar

4 eggs

1 teaspoon vanilla

Preparation

At 350 degrees F, preheat your oven. Grease a 13x9 inches baking pan. Mix the cottage cheese with the sugar, eggs, and vanilla in a bowl. Beat this mixture with an electric mixer until fluffy. Spread this mixture in the prepared pan and bake for 60 minutes until golden brown. Allow the cheese to cool and serve.

Kulich

Preparation time: 25 minutes
Cook time: 40 minutes
Nutrition facts (per serving): 586 Cal (21.9g fat, 12.4g protein, 2.5g fiber)

Without this Ukrainian Kulich, it seems like the Ukrainian dessert menu is incomplete. Try them with different variations of toppings besides the basic sugar glaze.

Ingredients (4 servings)

1 ½ (¼ oz) packages active dry yeast
¾ cup granulated sugar
1 cup warm milk
4 cups all-purpose flour
3 whole eggs, separated
2 large egg yolks
½ tablespoon brandy
½ teaspoon salt
10 tablespoons butter, melted and cooled
½ cup slivered blanched almonds, ground
¼ cup raisins
1 tablespoon water

Glaze

¾ cup confectioners' sugar
1 tablespoon lemon juice

Preparation

Mix ¼ teaspoon sugar, warm milk, and yeast in a large bowl and leave for 10 minutes. Add 1 ½ cups flour and mix well to make a dough. Cover the mixture with plastic wrap and leave for 1 hour. Beat all the 4 yolks with sugar for 3 minutes in a bowl until pale and foamy. Stir in the salt and the brandy. Mix the dough mixture and add butter and yolk mixture, then knead again. Beat the 3 egg whites in a mixer until they make soft peaks. Add the egg whites to the batter, along with 2 ½ cups flour, and then mix well. Cover it with plastic again and leave for 1 hour. Knead the inflated dough and add the raisins and the almonds and then knead until evenly incorporated. Grease 4 coffee cans with butter and divide the dough into the cans. Cover them with a kitchen towel and leave for 1 hour. At 350 degrees F, preheat the oven. Beat the remaining yolk with water in a bowl. Brush the top of the dough in the cans with yolk mixture and bake them for 40 minutes. Allow them to cool. Prepare the glaze by mixing powder sugar with lemon juice and pour over the loaves. Serve.

Traditional Donuts

Preparation time: 15 minutes
Cook time: 10 minutes
Nutrition facts (per serving): 347 Cal (5g fat, 7g protein, 5g fiber)

A dessert that has no parallel, the Ukrainian donuts are made with basic yeast dough to give you a delightful combination of flavors.

Ingredients (6 servings)
4 ½ teaspoon active dry yeast
1 ½ cups milk, warm
½ cup granulated sugar
½ cup butter
1 large egg
3 large egg yolks
1 tablespoon brandy
1 teaspoon salt
5 cups all-purpose flour
1 gallon vegetable oil for deep-frying
½ cup granulated sugar for rolling
1 cup jam for filling

Preparation
Mix the warm milk with yeast in a bowl and leave for 15 minutes. Stir in the sugar, butter, egg yolks, egg, brandy, and salt. Next, mix well. Stir in the rest of the ingredients and mix with a mixer using a dough hook until it makes a smooth dough. Cover the dough with plastic wrap and leave for 1 hour. Punch down the dough and spread it into ½ inch thick sheet, and cut a 3-inch round using a biscuit cutter. Reroll the

remaining dough and cut more rounds. Place the rounds in a tray, cover and leave for 30 minutes. Set a Dutch oven with oil and heat to 350 degrees F. Deep fry the donuts for 3 minutes per side until golden brown. Remove the donuts from the oil using a slotted spoon. Coat the donut with sugar and then poke a hole in the side of the donuts. Use a pastry bag to add the filling to the hole. Serve.

Khrustyky

Preparation time: 15 minutes
Cook time: 10 minutes
Nutrition facts (per serving): 83 Cal (4 g fat, 2 g protein, 0g fiber)

Yes, you can make something as delicious as this Ukrainian Khrustyky by using only basic dessert ingredients and some simple techniques.

Ingredients (6 servings)

2 large eggs
3 large egg yolks
1 tablespoon heavy whipping cream
1 tablespoon vanilla extract
2 tablespoon sugar
1-½ cups all-purpose flour
½ teaspoon salt
Oil for deep-fat frying
Confectioners' sugar

Preparation

Beat the eggs with vanilla, cream, and yolks in a large bowl. Stir in the flour, salt and sugar, and then mix well until smooth. Divide this dough into 4 portions. Roll out each dough piece into a ⅛-inch-thick sheet and cut each round into 3 (1 ½ inch) strips diagonally. Next, cut a 1 ½ inch slit at the center of each piece. Pull 1 end of the strip through the slit to make a loop. Cover the pieces and leave for 1 hour. Add the oil to a deep skillet and heat to 375 degrees F. Deep fry the dough loops until golden brown. Use a slotted spoon to plate lined with a paper towel. Dust them with sugar. Serve.

Ukrainian Cheesecake Tarts

Preparation time: 15 minutes

Cook time: 60 minutes

Nutrition facts (per serving): 357 Cal (12g fat, 5.5g protein, 1.4g fiber)

Try these cheesecake tarts on this special dessert menu. The sweet combination of butter, cheese, eggs, and basic flour tastes heavenly with jam filling.

Ingredients (6 servings)

⅓ cup butter melted

2 ½ cups cottage cheese

3 eggs

⅓ cup sugar

⅔ cup semolina flour

⅔ cup all-purpose flour

1 teaspoon vanilla extract

Various fruit jams, to taste

Preparation

Grease a muffin pan with butter. Mix all the remaining cheese and other ingredients in a bowl, except for the fruit jams, and then leave for 15 minutes. Divide this mixture into the muffin cups and bake for 1 hour at 325 degrees F in the oven. Serve.

Ukrainian Walnut Torte

Preparation time: 10 minutes
Cook time: 30 minutes
Nutrition facts (per serving): 425 Cal (17g fat, 5g protein, 0.8g fiber)

The Ukrainian walnut torte will leave you spellbound due to its mildly sweet taste, delicious filling, and mocha coating.

Ingredients (6 servings)

10 oz. walnuts

1 ¼ cup all-purpose flour

2 teaspoon cornstarch

1 teaspoon baking powder

12 large eggs

¼ teaspoon salt

1 ¼ cup granulated sugar

3 ½ teaspoon vanilla extract

¾ cup butter

Filling

6 oz. unsweetened chocolate, melted

6 ¼ cup sifted confectioners' sugar

¾ cup strongly brewed coffee

Mocha frosting

1 ½ tablespoon coffee liqueur

2 cup heavy cream

2 teaspoon instant-coffee granules

Preparation

Grease 2 (10 inches) round cake pans and grease with butter. Layer these pans with parchment paper. Mix the baking powder, cornstarch, flour, and walnuts in a bowl. Beat the egg whites with salt in a bowl until fluffy. Beat the egg yolks in a bowl at medium-high speed. Stir in sugar and beat for 5 minutes. Stir in 2 teaspoon of vanilla and mix well. Add the walnut mixture and egg whites and then mix well. Divide this batter into the pan and bake for 30 minutes. Allow the cakes to cool. Meanwhile, beat all the mocha frosting ingredients in a bowl. Prepared the filling by mixture its ingredients. Spread the filling on top of one cake, place the other cake on top, and garnish with the frosting. Slice and serve.

Ukrainian Kutia

Preparation time: 15 minutes
Cook time: 1 hour 30 minutes
Nutrition facts (per serving): 456 Cal (12g fat, 8g protein, 4g fiber)

The famous Ukrainian Kutia dessert is essential to try on the Ukrainian dessert menu. Cook it at home with these healthy ingredients and enjoy it.

Ingredients (6 servings)

9 oz. wheat berries
9 oz. poppy seeds
4 ½ cup milk
½ cup honey
3 ½ oz. almonds
3 oz. raisins
2 oz. cranberries
2 tablespoon candied orange peel
½ cup crème fraiche

Preparation

Soak the wheat berries in water overnight, then drain. Add the milk and the wheat berries to a pan and cook for 90 minutes. Stir in the poppy seeds and 3 cups water. Spread the nuts on a baking sheet and roast for 5 minutes. Drain the wheat berries and keep ½ cup milk aside. Mix the honey, the milk, and the orange juice in a bowl. Stir in the wheat berries and garnish with crème fraiche and toasted nuts. Serve.

Ukrainian Prune Torte

Preparation time: 5 minutes
Cook time: 30 minutes
Nutrition facts (per serving): 397 Cal (11g fat, 8g protein, 2g fiber)

The Ukrainian prune torte will make your day with their delightful taste. Serve fresh with some hot beverages.

Ingredients (6 servings)
Almond Cake
1 cup butter
1 cup confectioners' sugar
1 egg
½ teaspoon almond extract
1 pinch salt
¾ cup blanched almonds
2 cups sifted all-purpose flour

Prune Filling
16 oz. pitted prunes
1 cup water
1 cup white sugar
1 teaspoon ground cinnamon
1 tablespoon lemon juice

Preparation
At 350 degrees F, preheat your oven. Grease 5 (8inches) round pans with cooking oil. Blend all the almond cake ingredients in a food

processor. Divide the dough into 5 parts and roll each into an 8-inch round. Place each dough round in each pan and bake for 20 minutes. Mix the prunes and water and cook for 10 minutes, then drain. Blend the prunes with sugar, cinnamon, and lemon juice. Transfer to a pan and cook until it thickens. Spread this mixture in the baked crust. Serve.

Cheese Pockets

Preparation time: 15 minutes

Cook time: 25 minutes

Nutrition facts (per serving): 265 Cal (5g fat, 7g protein, 5g fiber)

A dessert that has no parallel, these cheese pockets can also be stuffed with other fillings like apple and cranberry mixes.

Ingredients (6 servings)

2 ½ cups flour

1 oz. yeast

2 tablespoon butter

1 egg

⅓ cup milk

2 tablespoon water

1 teaspoon sugar

1 egg yolk

1 teaspoon butter

Cheese Filling

1 lb. curd

1 egg

3 teaspoon sugar

Salt, to taste

Preparation

Beat the cheese filling ingredients in a bowl and keep it aside. Mix the yeast with lukewarm water and sugar in a bowl and leave for 5 minutes.

Stir in ½ cup flour and milk; then mix well to make smooth dough. Leave the dough for 15 minutes in a warm place. Add the remaining flour, and egg then mix well, then knead until smooth and elastic. Roll the dough on a floured surface onto a ½ inch thick sheet. Cut a 5-inch circle from this sheet. Press the center of the dough circles with the back of a spoon. Add 1 tablespoon cheese filling in the center of each circle. Place these circles on a baking sheet. Bake for 25 minutes at 350 degrees F. Serve.

Strawberry Cake

Preparation time: 15 minutes
Cook time: 35 minutes
Nutrition facts (per serving): 221 Cal (11g fat, 4g protein, 1.4g fiber)

This crusted Strawberry cake with whisk egg topping is the simplest recipe that you can try for your Ukrainian dessert menu.

Ingredients (10 servings)

2 eggs
½ cup sugar
5 oz. butter
2 cups flour
2 teaspoon baking powder
1 tablespoon vanilla powder
1 teaspoon lemon juice
1-lb. strawberries, quartered

Preparation

Divide the egg yolks and egg whites in two separate bowls. Add the sugar and ½ tablespoon vanilla powder to the egg yolks then beat well until sugar is completely dissolved. Stir in baking powder, flour, and soft butter. Mix well. Grease a suitable springform pan and spread the flour crust mixture at its base. Lightly press the crust and bake it at 355 degrees for 25 minutes. Meanwhile, blend the egg whites with ½ tablespoon vanilla powder a lemon juice until it is fluffy. Spread the strawberries onto the baked crust and top it with the egg white mixture. Bake for 10 minutes and then allow the dessert to cool. Slice and serve.

Plum Cake

Preparation time: 10 minutes

Cook time: 60 minutes

Nutrition facts (per serving): 317 Cal (17g fat, 5g protein, 0.8g fiber)

This plum cake has the softest texture and a chunky mix of plum on top. In turn, it not only looks great but also tastes divine!

Ingredients (8 servings)

2 cups flour

6 oz. butter

1 cup sugar

4 eggs

2 teaspoon baking powder

1 teaspoon vanilla powder

2 lb. plums

Powdered sugar and cinnamon

Preparation

Beat the butter with vanilla powder and sugar. Add the eggs, one by one, and continue beating the mixture until smooth until fluffy. Stir in the baking powder and flour; then mix until creamy. Grease a 10 inches baking pan with cooking spray. Spread the batter in the pan and top it with plums. Set the oven at 300 degrees F for preheating. Bake the cake for 1 hour and allow the cake to cool. Garnish with cinnamon and sugar. Slice and serve.

Ukrainian Cookies

Preparation time: 10 minutes
Cook time: 10 minutes
Nutrition facts (per serving): 202 Cal (7g fat, 6g protein, 1.3g fiber)

If you're a cookie lover, then this gingerbread cookie recipe is the right fit for you. Try this at home and cook in no time.

Ingredients (12 servings)

2 ½ cups flour
½ cup honey
4 tablespoon sugar
1 tablespoon butter
2 eggs
½ teaspoon baking powder
½ teaspoon clove powder
⅔ cup walnuts, chopped

Preparation

Heat the honey in a saucepan and add sugar. Remove this pan from its heat and add flour then mix well. Beat the eggs with baking powder, butter, clove powder, and chopped walnuts in a mixing bowl. Stir in the flour mixture and mix well until smooth and lump-free. Grease a baking sheet with cooking oil and drop the batter on the baking sheet, spoon by spoon, to make the cookies. Bake the cookies for 10 minutes at 390 degrees F. Allow the cookies to cool then serve.

Ukrainian Biscottis

Preparation time: 10 minutes
Cook time: 18 minutes
Nutrition facts (per serving): 393 Cal (18g g fat, 9g protein, 3g fiber)

Rich in nuts, apricots, and cherries, these biscotti are iconic on this menu. Try to serve them while fresh and crispy.

Ingredients (12 servings)
1 cup shelled almonds
1 cup shelled pistachios
⅓ cup canned pineapple, diced
⅓ cup dried apricots, diced
⅓ cup canned cherries
⅓ cup dried papaya
1 stick (8 tablespoon) butter, softened
1 cup granulated sugar
2 teaspoon vanilla extract
3 large eggs
3 ¼ cups all-purpose flour
2 ¼ teaspoon baking powder
¼ teaspoon salt

Preparation
Mix the baking powder, all-purpose flour, and salt in a mixing bowl. Beat the butter, eggs, sugar, and vanilla extract in another bowl. Pour this mixture into the flour mixture and then mix well until lump-free. Stir in the pineapple, apricots, cherries, papaya, almonds, and

pistachios. Mix well until it makes chunky dough. Divide the dough into 3 pieces and shape each of the dough pieces into 12x 12 inches logs from this mixture and then cut them into 1-inch biscotti. Place them on a baking sheet. Bake these biscotti for 18 minutes at 350 degrees F. Serve when cooled.

Spicy Cookies

Preparation time: 15 minutes
Cook time: 15 minutes
Nutrition facts (per serving): 181 Cal (6g fat, 2.4g protein, 0.6g fiber)

A dessert that has no parallel, these treats can also be served with delicious hot beverages as an evening snack.

Ingredients (6 servings)
1 ½ cup flour
½ cup honey
4 tablespoon sugar
¼ cup of water
3 ½ tablespoon butter
¼ lemon, juice, and zest
Pinch baking powder
1 egg yolk

Preparation
Add the water, sugar, and honey to a pan and cook the mixture to a boil and then remove it from the heat. Gradually stir in ½ of the flour and whisk well until smooth and lump-free. Stir in the lemon juice, lemon zest, baking powder, and butter. Mix well and add the remaining flour. Mix again until it makes smooth dough. Roll this dough on a lightly floured surface onto a ½ inch thick sheet. Use a cookie cutter to cut out the cookies. Place the cookies in a greased baking sheet. Brush the

cookies with the egg yolk. Bake the cookies for 15 minutes at 390 degrees F. Allow the cookies to cool then serve.

Drinks

Apple Kvass

Preparation time: 5 minutes

Cook time: 10 minutes

Nutrition facts (per serving): 112 Cal (0g fat, 4 protein, 3g fiber)

Beat the heat and try the famous Ukrainian Apple kvass with hints of coffee, apple cider, and apple juice. The combination is super refreshing and very healthy.

Ingredients (8 servings)

2 ½ gallons of water

4 teaspoon instant coffee

3 cups sugar

¾ cup apple cider vinegar

1 can (12 oz) apple juice

2 teaspoon yeast

Preparation

Add all the ingredients to a saucepan and cook to a boil. Remove the drink from the heat and allow it to ferment for 12 hours. Serve.

Kompot Drink

Preparation time: 5 minutes
Cook time: 15 minutes
Nutrition facts (per serving): 103 Cal (0g fat, 3g protein, 1g fiber)

The Ukrainian Kompot drink is loved by all due to its refreshing taste and sweet flavors. Serve it chilled for the best taste and flavor.

Ingredients (12 servings)
2 cup frozen strawberries
32 cups water
1 cup sugar

Preparation
Add the berries, sugar, and water to a saucepan and then cook for 15 minutes. Allow the drinks to cool, then drain, and serve.

Ukrainian Mulled Wine

Preparation time: 10 minutes
Cook time: 15 minutes
Nutrition facts (per serving): 130 Cal (1g fat, 0.4g protein, 5g fiber)

The Ukrainian mulled wine is great to serve on all special occasions and dinner, especially during the winter holidays.

Ingredients (4 servings)
3 cups dry white wine
½ cup orange juice
4 tablespoon brown sugar
6 cloves
1 teaspoon nutmeg grated
1 teaspoon cardamom ground
2 sticks cinnamon
½ cup medivka

Preparation
Add the wine and the rest of the ingredients to a saucepan and cook for 15 minutes on a simmer. Strain and serve.

Uzvar

Preparation time: 10 minutes
Cook time: 35 minutes
Nutrition facts (per serving): 167 Cal (1g fat, 4g protein, 5g fiber)

Uzvar is made from a nice blend of apples, pears, raisins, and prunes. It has a fruity rich flavor that tastes great when served chilled.

Ingredients (2 servings)
7 oz. dried apples
10 ½ oz. dried pears
3 ½ oz. raisins
7 oz. prunes
9 oz. honey
2 cups water

Preparation
Soak the dried fruits in cold water for 10 minutes and then rinse them. Boil the pears in boiling water and cook for 20 minutes. Stir in the raisins, prunes, and apples and then cook for 15 minutes. Add the honey, boil, and then remove from the heat. Allow the drink to cool, then serve.

Beetroot Drink

Preparation time: 10 minutes
Nutrition facts (per serving): 94 Cal (0g fat, 0.6g protein, 0g fiber)

A creamy mix of beetroot syrup and gin is all that you need to expand your Ukrainian menu. Simple and easy to make, this recipe is a must to try.

Ingredients (4 servings)

1 ½ oz. gin
⅔-oz. blackcurrant puree
⅓-oz. beetroot syrup
⅓-oz. Lemon Juice
⅔-oz. egg white

Preparation

Blend the gin, blackcurrant puree, beetroot syrup, lemon juice, and egg white in a blender. Refrigerate for 1 hour. Serve.

If you liked Ukrainian recipes, discover to how cook DELICIOUS recipes from **Balkan** countries!

Within these pages, you'll learn 35 authentic recipes from a Balkan cook. These aren't ordinary recipes you'd find on the Internet, but recipes that were closely guarded by our Balkan mothers and passed down from generation to generation.

Main Dishes, Appetizers, and Desserts included!

If you want to learn how to make Croatian green peas stew, and 32 other authentic Balkan recipes, then start with our book!

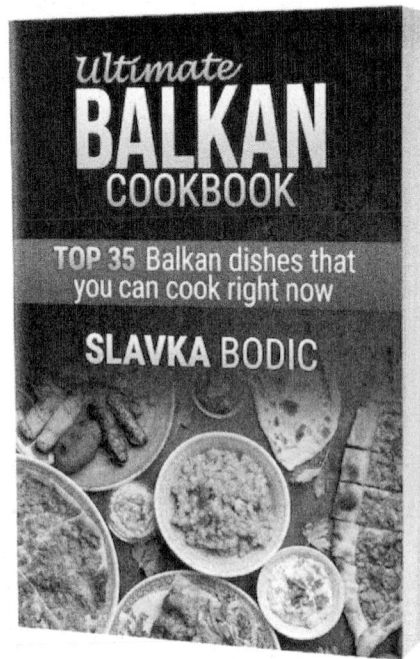

Order at www.balkanfood.org/cook-books/ for only $2,99!

Maybe Hungarian cuisine?

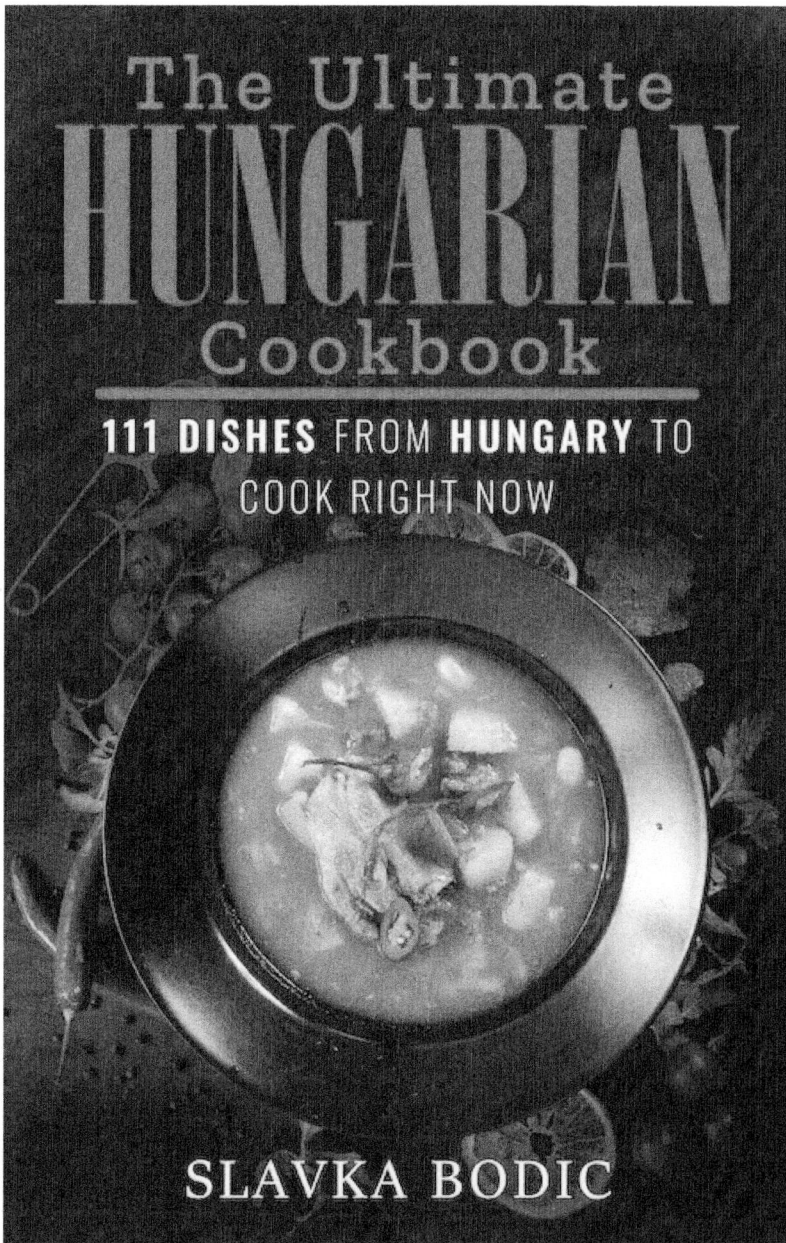

If you're a **Mediterranean** dieter who wants to know the secrets of the Mediterranean diet, dieting, and cooking, then you're about to discover how to master cooking meals on a Mediterranean diet right now!

In fact, if you want to know how to make Mediterranean food, then this new e-book - "The 30-minute Mediterranean diet" - gives you the answers to many important questions and challenges every Mediterranean dieter faces, including:

- How can I succeed with a Mediterranean diet?
- What kind of recipes can I make?
- What are the key principles to this type of diet?
- What are the suggested weekly menus for this diet?
- Are there any cheat items I can make?

... and more!

If you're serious about cooking meals on a Mediterranean diet and you really want to know how to make Mediterranean food, then you need to grab a copy of "The 30-minute Mediterranean diet" right now.

Prepare **111 recipes with several ingredients in less than 30 minutes**!

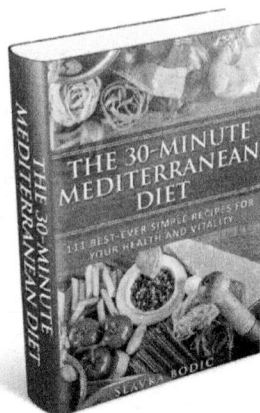

Order at www.balkanfood.org/cook-books/ for only $2,99!

What could be better than a home-cooked meal? Maybe only a **Greek** homemade meal.

Do not get discouraged if you have no Greek roots or friends. Now you can make a Greek food feast in your kitchen.

This ultimate Greek cookbook offers you 111 best dishes of this cuisine! From more famous gyros to more exotic *Kota Kapama* this cookbook keeps it easy and affordable.

All the ingredients necessary are wholesome and widely accessible. The author's picks are as flavorful as they are healthy. The dishes described in this cookbook are "what Greek mothers have made for decades."

Full of well-balanced and nutritious meals, this handy cookbook includes many vegan options. Discover a plethora of benefits of Mediterranean cuisine, and you may fall in love with cooking at home.

Inspired by a real food lover, this collection of delicious recipes will taste buds utterly satisfied.

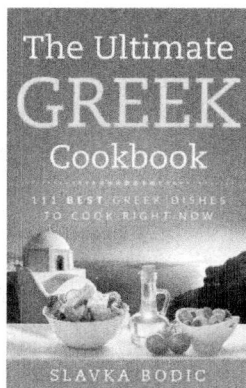

Order at www.balkanfood.org/cook-books/ for only $2,99!

Maybe some Swedish meatballs ?

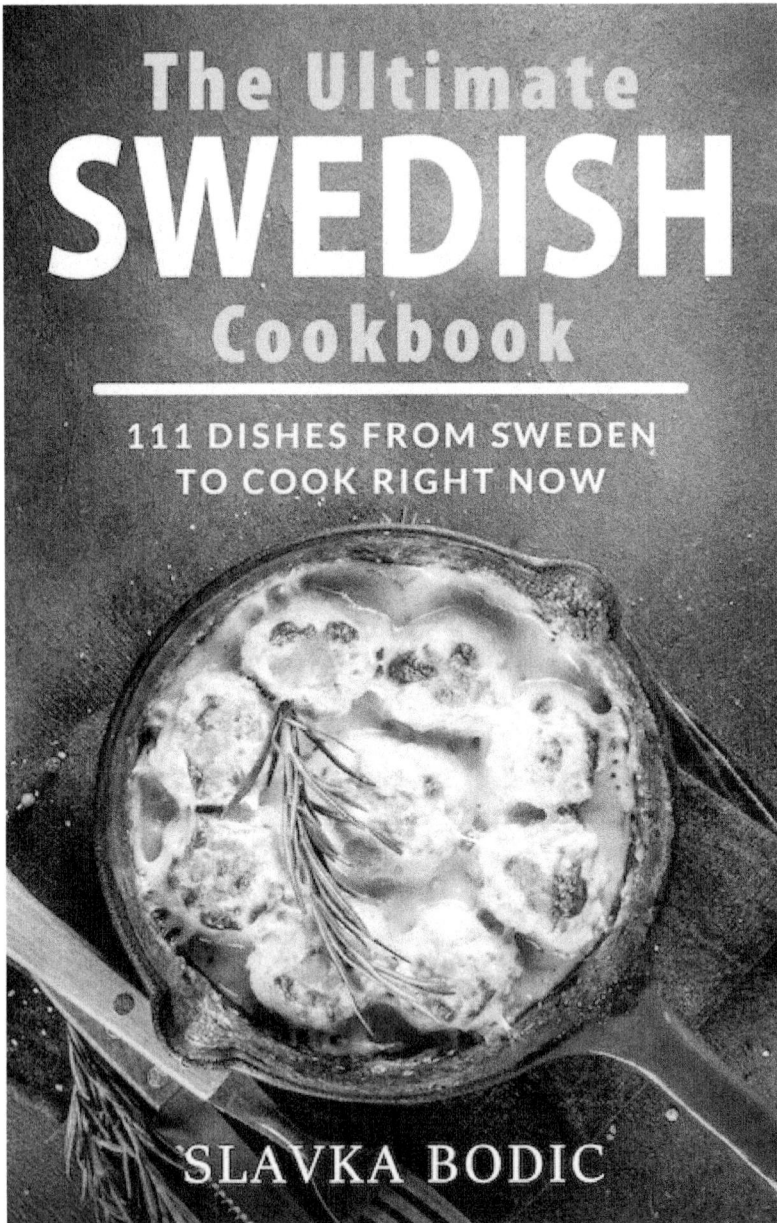

Order at www.balkanfood.org/cook-books/ for only $2,99!

Maybe to try exotic **Syrian** cuisine?

From succulent *sarma*, soups, warm and cold salads to delectable desserts, the plethora of flavors will satisfy the most jaded foodie. Have a taste of a new culture with this **traditional Syrian cookbook**.

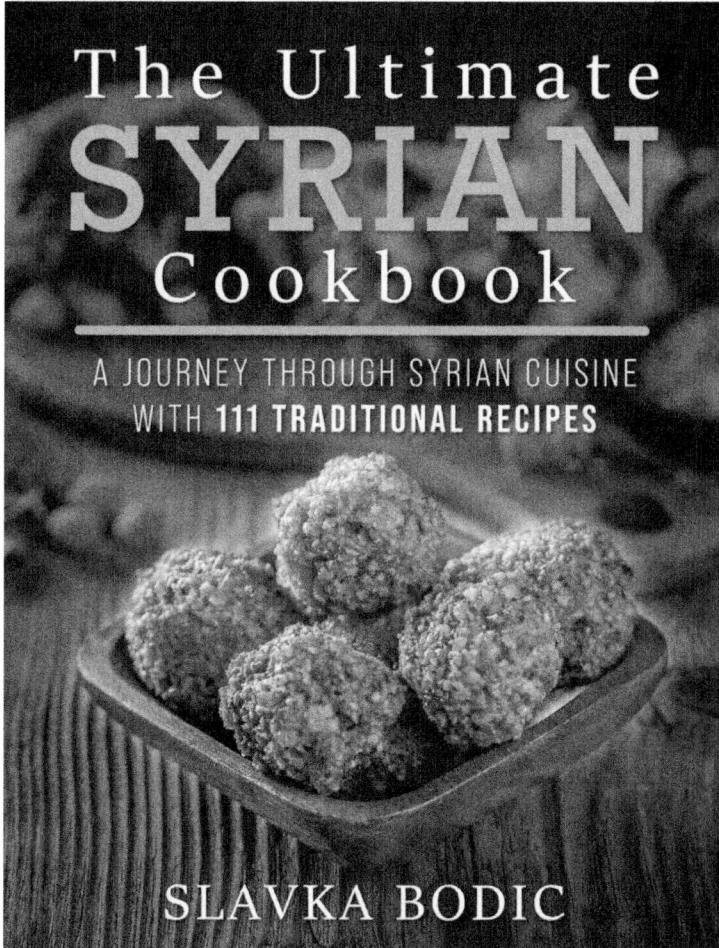

Maybe **Polish** cuisine?

Order at www.balkanfood.org/cook-books/ for only $2,99!

Or **Peruvian**?

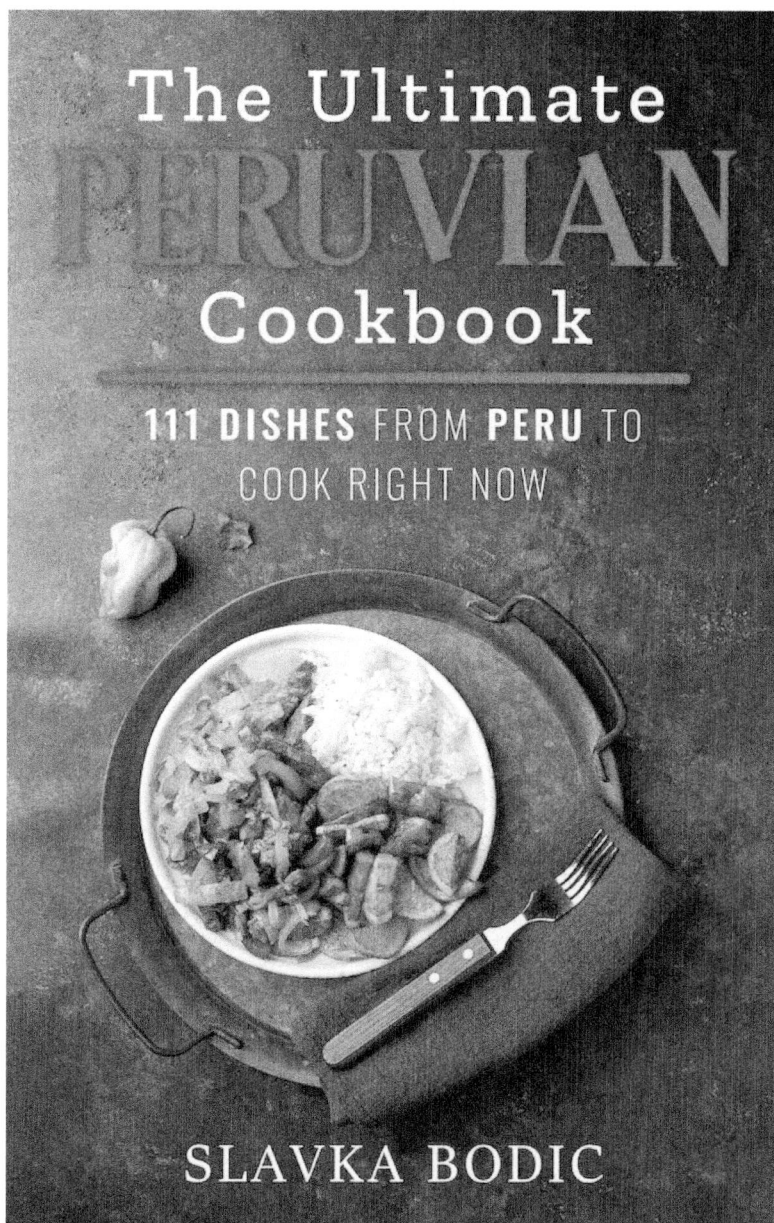

ONE LAST THING

If you enjoyed this book or found it useful, I'd be very grateful if you could find the time to post a short review on Amazon. Your support really does make a difference and I read all the reviews personally, so I can get your feedback and make this book even better.

Thanks again for your support!

Please send me your feedback at

www.balkanfood.org

Printed in Great Britain
by Amazon